DOUBLE BILL

Alec McCowen
DOUBLE BILL

Atheneum

NEW YORK

1980

B
M

Contents

Acknowledgements

The publishers gratefully acknowledge the following for permission to reproduce copyright photographs and illustrations: T. F. Holte (1); BBC (3, 14, 30); John Haynes (6); Peter Mitchell, Camera Press Ltd (7, 11, 13, 15); Jill Krementz (9, 17); Cecil Beaton, courtesy of Sotheby's Belgravia (12); The Press International Inc. (18, 20); © 1969 by The New York Times Company (19); Zoe Dominic (22, 25, 29); Nobby Clarke (31); Arnold Weisberger (34); Arthur Cantor (32, b, c, d); Donald Cooper (32a). Every effort has been made to trace the copyright holders of the photographs used in this volume. Should there be any omissions in this respect, we apologise and shall be pleased to make the appropriate acknowledgement in future editions.

Illustrations

DOUBLE BILL

INTRODUCTION

The trouble with most 'show-business' memoirs is that they usually consist of an interminable list of credits.

And then I wrote . . .

And then I composed . . .

And then I played . . .

And when the author is an actor, the temptation to put in every performance in every play, and every movie, and every television, and every broadcast, seems irresistible, until the reader is bludgeoned with titles and dates, and carefully selected excerpts from reviews, and dazzled with a kaleidoscope of success and failure.

I have tried to avoid this pattern.

And failed.

Or anyway, partly failed.

This book is a description of only two productions, *Hadrian VII* and my own solo performance of St Mark's Gospel, and there is a gap of several years in the writing of these two stories. On both occasions I have written about the preparatory work, the rehearsals, the reactions of audiences, the adventures, the fun and the exhaustion. The adventures of an actor on two occasions in his career when the odds were against him.

The first story begins when I was thirty-nine and at a low ebb in my life. This story leads to the play *Hadrian VII* produced three years later at the Mermaid Theatre, London, followed by a season in America.

The second story begins when I was forty-nine and at a low ebb in my life. This story leads to my solo performance of St Mark's Gospel produced – by an extraordinary coincidence – three years later at the Mermaid Theatre, London, followed by a season in America.

Using this skeleton as a basis, I have written about many aspects of an actor's life along the way.

And in both stories I seem to mention as many of my performances in plays, and films, and television, and broadcasts, as I can – in order to impress my colleagues and my readers that I have a list of credits as long as anyone else's, a large selection of excerpts from carefully selected reviews, and a seasoned acquaintance with that dazzling kaleidoscope of failure and success.

Hadrian VII

HADRIAN VII

I have appeared in many plays, and many of them have stories attached to them, but *Hadrian VII* is perhaps the most dramatic story.

The play has a Cinderella theme. Poor persecuted Cinders achieves her dream, goes to the ball and marries Prince Charming. In *Hadrian VII* poor persecuted Freddy Rolfe achieves his dream, goes to the Vatican and becomes Pope. But the adventure of the progress of the play itself is also a Cinderella story. For years it was rejected by managements and leading actors. For years it was unrecognized and gathered dust. It was considered uncommercial and impractical, and the role of Hadrian considered unplayable. Even after its first production in Birmingham, where it played to half empty houses, it seemed unlikely that *Hadrian* would ever achieve its subsequent astonishing international success. Only after the London production, almost a year later, did the critics wave their magic wands, and the unexpected miracle occurred. The rare phenomenon of 'overnight success', which tempts madmen to spend their lives in the ridiculous profession of show-business, actually happened and actors, authors, directors and producers looked on with excitement and relief. Dreams can come true.

*

As far as I am concerned, the story begins in 1964.

1964 was a fairly unpleasant year for me. I was a thirty-nine-year-old character-juvenile actor, and I was playing what is perhaps the most testing part for an actor of that type – the Fool in *King Lear*. It seemed to me strangely like the end of the road. At the Old Vic, I had played Touchstone in *As You Like It*, the Dauphin in *St Joan*, Algy in *The Importance of Being Earnest* and Mercutio in *Romeo and Juliet*. I had also played many showy supporting parts in contemporary West End productions – such

5

as the schoolboy, Daventry, in Roger MacDougall's *Escapade*, Barnaby, the young apprentice, in Thornton Wilder's *The Matchmaker*, and I had a success as the rebellious son in T. S. Eliot's last play *The Elder Statesman*. But it was obvious that, as I approached forty, this line of characters would no longer come my way. I was too old to go on playing neurotic youngsters, or charming but stunted Peter Pan personalities. Only Buttons in pantomime seemed to be left. I was bored with my work and afraid of the future.

With Paul Scofield in *King Lear*

There was also another strange hang-up. For years I had been haunted by tales told of the legendary young actor, Stephen Haggard, who died during the 1939–45 war. Haggard had played many of the plum character-juvenile roles in the West End during the thirties and, on several occasions, I found myself being compared with him. I felt an odd kinship with his life and his career. His last performance was as the Fool in *Lear*. With a perverse actor's death-wish I thought perhaps it would also be mine.

In any case I knew it would be ultimate disaster for me to go

on playing, as I usually did, parts much younger than myself –
and trading on a youthful appearance until the day my hair fell
out. Already I was having to brown in a bald spot and shade
away a sagging chin. There is nothing sadder than an 'old
juvenile'.

In Belgrade with the *King Lear* company – John Laurie on my left and Paul Scofield
in the centre – meeting Marshal Tito

During the early months of 1964 – having just finished a most
gruelling role in Rolf Hochhuth's play *The Representative* – I set
off with the Royal Shakespeare Company on a tour of Eastern
Europe and America, playing the Fool to Paul Scofield's King
Lear in Peter Brook's famous production, and Antipholus of
Syracuse in Clifford Williams's equally successful production of
The Comedy of Errors. Before the tour started, I was tired and
depressed. Then, in the first eight weeks, we visited Berlin,
Prague, Budapest, Belgrade, Bucharest, Warsaw, Helsinki,
Leningrad and Moscow. I found the demands made were very
great. In addition to playing two heavy roles, there were many
extra recitals of Shakespeare which we gave to universities, old

people's homes and drama schools. There were interminable receptions where we had to be gracious to Embassy and British Council officials, and encouraging to the local theatrical scene. Hotel and dressing-room accommodation were often badly arranged, and I was not happy in the company. Of course it was a joy to work with Scofield; there was the beautiful and witty Diana Rigg; the ravishing young Julie Christie; and I spent a lot of my time with that splendid veteran Scots actor, John Laurie. He and I always sat together on planes, and on arrival in Leningrad, we rushed off to the Hermitage to find the great collection of Impressionist paintings tucked away on the top floor.

On the last day in Moscow, after visiting Lenin's Tomb, the State School for Circus Artists, a press reception, a reception for the Minister of Culture, a reception for Mr Mikoyan, and a performance of *The Comedy of Errors*, I heard that there was a further reception with the British Ambassador and I fled from the company and ran through the snowy streets to Red Square, where I stood in peace under the electric red stars of the Kremlin. Two young Russians approached and, in halting English, begged for a cigarette. I gave them the packet and we talked together. They asked me about night life in the West and whether all the women looked like Marilyn Monroe. I told them comfortingly that many Russian women seemed equally well built. They were unconvinced. Then, after looking carefully round the deserted square, one of them whispered, 'At home I have a copy of *Playboy* magazine.' 'Where did you get it?' I asked loudly. He begged me to be silent and once more looked round the huge empty square. Our conversation moved on to safer topics. I suggested coffee – but it was after eleven and everything was shut. I suggested they came back to my hotel for a drink, but they said – quite simply and without complaint – 'It would not be good for us to be seen with you there.' So they found me a taxi and we parted.

The next day the company flew to Washington, and I spent a glorious weekend – living alone at the Willard Hotel, eating ham and eggs, drinking bourbon, watching television and walking through the cherry blossom. The tawdry joys of capitalism seemed very very sweet: neon signs, canned music, and unlimited pornography. But there was one extraordinary similarity. In Moscow there was the long queue to the Tomb of Lenin, and in Washington there was the long queue to the new grave of President Kennedy.

However, despite the fact that during the American part of the tour there was more privacy and leisure time, the strain of the performances was increased because we played in huge theatres to audiences far less sympathetic than in Europe. The final disappointment came when we opened the brand new Lincoln State Theatre in New York. Rehearsing in an empty auditorium the acoustics seemed perfect, but on the first night of *King Lear*, with a full house it seemed impossible to make oneself heard. And, as my friend Gil Parker said when he came backstage after the performance, 'It's not as if there was anything to look at!' A couple of nights later we screamed out *The Comedy of Errors* but it was not much better.

I had been working in these two plays for over eighteen months and was heartily sick of both of them. I felt completely played out and thought that I would never want to act again. We flew back to England in June and gave a Command Performance of '*The Comedy*' to the entire Royal Family and their Ascot guests at Windsor Castle. It was a glamorous occasion – but I was relieved when it was over and to know that I would never wear that costume and wig again.

There followed a gloomy six months during which I turned down work and tried to do some writing. Personal affairs were going badly, and the lease on my Chelsea flat was not renewed. It was necessary to find a new home. I was offered a leading part with the Royal Shakespeare Company in a play at the Aldwych – but it was another frenetic character-juvenile personality and I turned it down. The only happy event was a crazy week in Rome playing the tiny part of a spiteful Cardinal in a movie called *The Agony and the Ecstasy*. This involved climbing some scaffolding in a studio reproduction of the Sistine Chapel and shouting at Charlton Heston who, as Michelangelo, was busy painting a nude on the ceiling: 'Obscenity! Filth and obscenity!' The director, Carol Reed, spent three days shooting the scene, but in the final cut I was hardly in evidence and it mainly consisted of a close-up of Charlton Heston listening to me. However, during the week I enjoyed the marvellous companionship of Richard Pearson – happily playing a fellow Cardinal – and I met Rex Harrison, who had the unlikely role of Pope. (Richard and I had a memorable evening with Rex Harrison – for years an idol of

9

mine – in his villa on the Appian Way. Knowing him to be a fanatical perfectionist, I asked if there was any one performer whom he particularly admired. 'Fred Astaire,' he said. It made absolute sense.)

I moved to an ugly new flat in Notting Hill Gate and spent a horrible time decorating and furnishing. My nerves were in a shocking state and I seemed to have lost my confidence. Then my good friend and agent, Philip Pearman, died suddenly, and there followed the unpleasant but necessary task of finding other representation.

I joined Dennis Van Thal's organization and he introduced me to a smiling Scotsman called Larry Dalzell. Larry seemed eager to look after me. We had a talk in his office and I told him of my dilemma as a middled-aged juvenile, and of my determination to break away from my old line of wide-eyed boys and chippy neurotics. He seemed to understand and mentioned three plays he knew of which were awaiting production. The one he liked best was called *Hadrian VII*. It didn't sound very promising to me. A man imagines he's the Pope – and then in the end discovers it was all a dream. Too often in the past had I heard those groans of disgust from audiences at films and plays where they have been fooled into thinking something had occurred which was actually fantasy. However, I liked Larry and decided to join him, and he urged me to read *Hadrian* when he could get hold of a copy.

I started to work again, on television. First there was a domestic play by Peter Nichols with Eileen Atkins. Then a political comedy by Simon Raven. After this I went to Birmingham for two months, inventing the telephone in a six-part serial of the life of Alexander Graham Bell. Then I was offered a TV production in the title role of John Osborne's *Luther*. This was the heaviest part I had ever played and I felt I was making some progress towards the future. But television is not fully satisfying and I was restless to get back to the stage.

On my fortieth birthday Laurier Lister, the director of productions at the new Yvonne Arnaud Theatre at Guildford, rang and asked me if I would like to play the Ralph Lynn part in Ben Travers's classic farce, *Thark*. This was not what I was looking for, but I couldn't resist the challenge of working in a farce – perhaps the most difficult of all the dramatic mediums – and I gladly accepted. It was a refreshing and exhausting

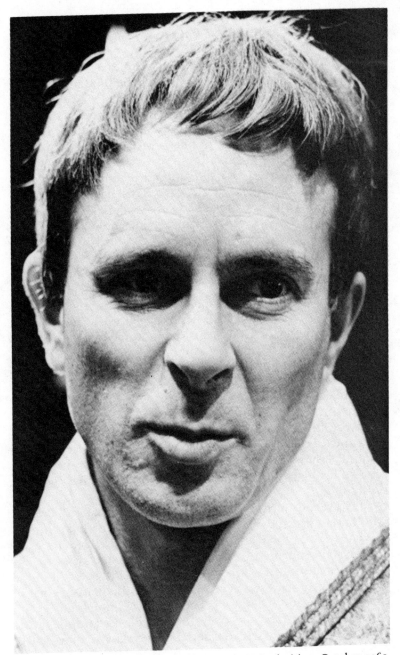

Celebrating my first Mass as Martin Luther – BBC television, October 1965

experience. I found the energy and concentration required to perform the most ridiculous situations with absolute reality and speed greater than anything I'd ever done before. Also I had never expected to find myself sleeping with Peter Cushing and complaining to him: 'Oh you are awful in bed!' as we tugged at the sheets in the famous ghost scene.

Round about the same time as *Thark*, I was asked to take part in a Sunday charity performance called *Homage to T. S. Eliot*. There was another instance of unexpected incongruity when I entered the theatre and looked at the dressing-room list – which was arranged alphabetically – and discovered my name next to Groucho Marx. He was reading Eliot's 'Gus the Theatre Cat'. It was a triumphant but nerve-racking evening. Other readers included Sir Laurence Olivier, Paul Scofield and Peter O'Toole. I was lucky to be allotted two very fine poems and, as a result, the impresario Hugh (Binkie) Beaumont thought of offering me a part in a new play he was planning to put on in the autumn. This turned out to be exactly what I was hoping for.

It was the part of the Author – Anouilh himself – in his play *The Cavern*. I left the cast of *Thark* a few weeks after it had transferred to the Garrick Theatre, and started my new career as a middle-aged actor.

In order to look like Anouilh, I had a grey wig made, found the appropriate spectacles and stuck on a moustache. I had the enjoyable role of a man in authority, often interrupting the other actors with my comments, and complaining directly to the audience about the play I had supposedly written. It was a witty idea and an immensely theatrical play – but the great vogue for Anouilh seemed to be over. We toured the provinces to empty houses for eight weeks, and struggled for only four weeks in London.

It is a very dispiriting experience to be in a flop – especially if you have a great love and respect for the play you are doing. Perhaps on the first night, and on a Saturday, you get a full house and hear the sort of reaction that the play deserves, but for the majority of performances, there is that awful empty feeling which depresses everyone involved. Laugh-lines get no laughs, dramatic surprises get no gasps, curtain calls get no applause – and in the back of one's mind is the knowledge that the day is fast approaching when the termination notice will go up on the board, and there will not only be no laughs, no gasps and no applause, but no money and no job. Actors whisper together, 'Have you heard anything?' 'Is there any advance?' 'Why isn't there more publicity?' And when there is an unexpectedly good house the cynics murmur, 'I'm sure it's only paper,' inferring that the management have given away complimentary tickets to fill the embarrassing rows of empty seats and impress the paying customers.

The cynics are usually right. (It is a great complaint among actors that managements seldom give complimentary tickets to *them* when a play is doing badly. They are fondly supposed not to notice, and it is hoped that they will foster the illusion that the play is a success. This is quite different in America where the trade paper, *Variety*, which is sold on every news-stand, publishes the weekly box-office figures of all the plays on Broadway and on tour – usually accompanied by pithy comments such as 'Slipping', 'Climbing', 'Sleepy' or 'Socko'.)

After the failure of *The Cavern*, the Royal Shakespeare Company beckoned again, this time with another Fool: Feste in *Twelfth Night*. But I was determined to persevere in my new career as long as I could afford it. In any case, a return to the strain of making contemporary audiences laugh at obscure Elizabethan jokes – combined with the horror of living in Stratford – did not tempt me. My New Year's resolution for 1966 was: 'I will no longer play the fool – privately or professionally'. . . but apart from turning down Feste, I did not sustain it with much success.

Some time during the past year I must have read *Hadrian VII* – although I do not remember the occasion – for my diary records on 4 February: 'Re-read *Hadrian*, the play based on Fr Rolfe's life and novel. Very nearly very good.'

Then, on 13 February, I made the following surprising entry:

Started to think about the play *Hadrian* in the middle of the night and woke myself up to a pitch of absurd feverish excitement – just as I used to dream of Hollywood and becoming a great film star when I was a schoolboy. The performance, of course, outshone the play and was the prime reason for its success. Interviews on television and in the newspapers followed. I even started to speculate where I

13

would live during the ensuing New York season, and the problem of finding another part as good when it finally closed – I hope other people do this!

But a month later, on 12 March, I simply wrote: 'Looked at *Hadrian* – which might get done in the summer. A lot of it is totally undramatic and looks impossible.'

Nevertheless, I went on reading it at frequent intervals and pondering its chances of success; but there was always the same reaction. Immense excitement over Act One; then a cooling of excitement, followed by boredom and depression over Act Two – which I seldom managed even to finish – and a resumption of enthusiasm over Act Three. It had to be faced, that a play that sent you to sleep or to make a cup of coffee when you reached its middle, was not quite right, and that it needed to be cut and radically reconstructed. However, Larry Dalzell continued to believe in it, and I met the producer, Bill Freedman, who held an option on the play with his partner, Charles Kasher.

Bill arranged a discussion with me, Peter Luke the playwright, and Charles Jarrot, who was interested in directing it. We all had too many ideas, most of them contradictory. It must have been a depressing experience for Peter Luke, who had achieved the astonishing feat of wresting a drama out of the life of Rolfe, and merging it with the novel of *Hadrian VII*. But he was unfailingly courteous, although by the end of the evening the future of the play looked as uncertain as ever.

In the meantime I went back to television; playing in a dramatization of E. M. Forster's *Where Angels Fear to Tread*, with Wendy Hiller and my dear friend, Anna Massey; a disastrous production of Aldous Huxley's *Ape and Essence*; and giving a highly neurotic performance in T. S. Eliot's *The Family Reunion*.

The complications encountered in a TV studio are legion, and it doesn't do to take yourself too seriously. Wendy Hiller – a wonderful and dedicated actress – asked me, when we were trying to remember our carefully rehearsed performances in *Where Angels Fear to Tread* during the chaos of the camera day: 'Alec, I've been asked to *approach* the hotel by walking *away* from it. Can you give me a motivation?' I couldn't!

In *The Family Reunion*, as Harry, Lord Monchensey, the unhappy and haunted hero, I made my first dramatic entry into the drawing-room and drew the curtains so violently that the entire window collapsed and the recording was suspended while the carpenter wagged his finger at me and said 'Naughty!'

And years ago in a live transmission of a complicated little play, which included among its sets an office block and a duck pond in a park complete with live ducks, I played a highly dramatic scene in the office with a stray duck on the filing cabinet.

A glossy publicity still with Joan Fontaine in *The Witches*

I was also offered another 'bread and butter' job during this time – in a Hammer horror movie called *The Witches*. I gladly accepted, although the role was ignominious. As the cowardly brother of a witch, I was required to wear a dog-collar – although the character was not connected with the church – and retire to my study playing organ music on a tape-recorder whenever my sister got on to her broomstick. The heroine of the film was played by the glamorous Hollywood star, Joan Fontaine. As the village school-mistress, she gallantly vanquished my sister and in the last reel even managed to make a man of me. However, I was very grateful to Hammer Films during the next year, as my salary from *The Witches* subsidized a very meagre income from the theatre.

By a marvellous stroke of good fortune, but a maddening coincidence, two plays came on offer to me in the summer of 1966 – both with the type of 'heavy' part that I was wanting. A choice had to be made.

Vivian Matalon

The first play was *After the Rain* and was to be done at the Hampstead Theatre Club. The other play, to be done at the Dublin Festival, was *Hadrian VII*. *After the Rain* seemed to me to be the better play – although *Hadrian VII* had a more obviously virtuoso leading role. *After the Rain* had the additional attraction that it was written by an old friend, John Bowen, and was to be directed by another old friend, Vivian Matalon. Vivian has taught me more about acting than anyone else in the theatre – although, until then, we had never had the opportunity of working together professionally as actor and director. But for many years during rehearsals of countless plays I had gone to him for help when I was confused, and invariably he had clarified the problems and set me on the right, active and energetic lines. As a director, he has a genius for analysis and selection. As a friend, he is a joyous and hilarious companion. With very little regret I turned down *Hadrian VII* and assumed, as far as I was concerned, that that would be the end of it. Luckily for me they were not able to cast another actor, and its production was once again postponed.

With Maureen Pryor in *After the Rain*

At the Hampstead Theatre Club we had a sensational success with *After the Rain*. The reviews were magnificent. For its short two-week run the theatre was besieged by ecstatic admirers and completely sold out. Probably, if we had continued to run at Hampstead, we could have played to full houses for a year. In New York, a successful off-Broadway show usually stays in its original little theatre – but this is not the London way. Plans were made for us to transfer to the West End, but at the time there was no suitable theatre vacant. It was not until four months later, in January 1967, that we reopened at the Duchess Theatre. By then the sensation had worn off. Although the notices were again very good, the surprise of the original production was dissipated. The weather was freezing and, understandably, the public was not attracted to a play described by a leading critic as 'a sleet-storm of icy wit and intelligence'. Even my own performance was described as 'chilling'.

Once again one had the depressing experience of glimpsing those empty rows of seats. Once again the actors started to whisper. And once again – after a four-month wait for a West End theatre without any pay – the company started to worry about money and the next job. With the producers, the director and the author, I took a salary cut, but it was no use. After eight weeks of appalling business, we closed. The only bright hope was the enthusiasm of a petite, blonde American called Helen Jacobson, who was determined to take the play to New York in the autumn – with as many of the original company as American Equity would allow.

Almost immediately after the London opening, when it already looked extremely doubtful that we would succeed at the box-office, my agent, Larry Dalzell, telephoned to discuss a possible April production of *Hadrian VII* at the Birmingham Repertory Theatre. I was very bad tempered at his inference that *After the Rain* would fail and refused to discuss it. He then asked me simply if he could tell the producers that, if a production was set up, I would be interested in playing the part. I grumpily agreed. Then I discussed it with a few friends.

My part in *After the Rain* was that of a fanatical bespectacled little man who imagined that he was God. When friends asked me about my part in *Hadrian VII*, I could only reply, 'A fanatical bespectacled little man who imagines that he is Pope.' Friends said emphatically, 'No! Don't do it!' Quite apart from the fact that it boded another box-office disaster, the move from God to Pope was a come-down.

I re-read the play for the hundredth time – and for the hundredth time my mind wandered off in Act Two and I found myself reading the *Radio Times*. Then I picked up the play again and for the hundredth time became enthralled with Act Three. Suddenly the answer seemed quite simple. Cut as much of Act Two as possible, and put the play into two acts with only one interval.

I made notes of what I thought should be specifically cut; then I went to see Larry. With unusual firmness I told him that I would only agree to do the play if these alterations to the script were made. Luckily, Peter Dews – who was now to direct the play

– thought that the change from three acts to two acts was an improvement; and patient Peter Luke agreed to perform the painful surgery.

There were a few weeks to wait. I began to get excited. Since the character is supposed to be starving, I went on a diet, which had the side-effect of making me so energetic that one day I climbed right up to the Golden Ball on top of St Paul's Cathedral – surely a very appropriate physical preparation.

I bought some dreadful pink-rimmed National Health spectacles, and had my third consecutive grey wig made.

I started to make notes on the character – of a somewhat general nature judging by a reminder which I see in an early script: 'Hadrian's a pouf.'

Finally I found a quotation of Rolfe's in *The Quest for Corvo* which seemed to be the very essence of the man. 'I cultivate the gentle art of making enemies. A friend is necessary, one friend – but an enemy is more necessary. An enemy keeps one alert.' This became my text.

On 13 April I travelled by train to Birmingham with Peter Luke. We were both astonished that the first day of rehearsal had actually arrived. I checked in at the Albany Hotel, had lunch there alone, and then walked over to the theatre.

Birmingham

Sometimes memory remains as vivid as reality. Sometimes it is hazy, and sometimes one forgets altogether.

I remember vividly going up the stairs, alone, to the director's office backstage at the Birmingham Repertory Theatre, for that first reading of *Hadrian*. Steeling myself to meet new people, a new company, and feeling the dreadful uncertainty of my ability to speak a line of dialogue with any expression – or even sense. Feeling lonely, ill-advised, and inadequate. Feeling my throat dry and the muscles of my face twitch as I prepared to smile and meet the company. Failing to feel the comfort of past experience, feeling exposed, afraid and, above all, stupid. Why am I daring to do this? Why don't I drive a taxi, cut hair, or sell cigarettes?

I opened a door and faced a circle of about twenty disconcertingly young faces. 'Hello!' I said. 'Hello!' some of them replied. 'Is this the right place for the read-through?' I asked, rather as if I was boarding a train for an unknown destination. 'Yes,' some of them answered. I found a chair and sat down, looking around at my fellow passengers. Some of them smiled, and others continued their conversations. I opened my script as if I had never seen it before, and pretended to search for something in the dialogue. One of the company leaned over and asked if I remembered him; we had met briefly at Stratford some years before. I said 'Ah yes!' and 'How are you?' as if he was a long-lost brother – and wondered if his hair was dyed. Then Peter Dews, the director, bustled in. 'Ah, I see you've met the Pope,' he said to the company, and greeted me – smiling like a mischievous schoolboy.

Usually on these occasions one looks at a model of the set, and inspects the designs for the costumes. The costume designs were handed round, but Peter explained that, owing to the expense and technical difficulties of staging a play that moves quickly in scene from a shabby bed-sitter to the Vatican, he had decided to abandon the realistic set designs and work on a completely bare stage – using only such furniture and trappings as were absolutely vital to the play. In the Birmingham production we used only two chairs and a screen for the scenes in my lodgings, and a huge throne for the scenes in the Vatican. Entrances were made either direct from the wings, or from under the stage and up some winding iron stairs at the back. In subsequent productions in London and New York, the scenery got a little more elaborate – but I always liked the complete simplicity of the original, imposed by the economic and physical obstacles of the little Birmingham Rep. The lack of space backstage also inspired Peter to have the great entrance of the Cardinals through the auditorium. There was no other way to get them on. This became one of the most splendid theatrical moments of the production. Perhaps if we had been working in ideal conditions it would never have happened, and a great *coup de théâtre* would have been lost.

Although there was no scenery, the designs for the costumes were superb and extravagant. Most of them were being made by the theatre wardrobe, but specialities like my white robes were made by the leading Catholic clerical tailors, who were thrilled to have this unique opportunity to dress a Pope.

We made appreciative mooing noises as we looked at the designs, and I made a private mental note that I would never wear the wide-brimmed hat with the tassels; I might look like Arthur Askey in a Mexican Western. I also worried that Hadrian's white costume would pick up too much light, obscure my face and tire the eyes of the audience. Perhaps it should be made in cream . . .

The reading began. I seemed to have very little control over my voice and decided to read it quite flatly. It wasn't until Act Two that a line burst out with a savagery that surprised me – and startled the company. Peter winked and I blushed. After the reading we had a cup of tea, and that evening I went to see the company in a lively production of *As You Like It*.

I remember very little about the three-week rehearsal period of *Hadrian* at Birmingham, except the three 'run-throughs' of the play. The usual procedure of most directors is first to 'block' the play in a physical sense – which may take as much as a week – and then to work slowly through each scene in detail, examining the text and discovering as much as possible about the characters and their actions. Then, when this has been

Having tea on Hadrian's throne during a rehearsal at the Mermaid – 1968

completed, comes the first run-through of the play; the actors working without scripts and the director sitting out front. It is a traditionally nerve-racking occasion and the performance is often a shambles. Words and moves are not accurately learnt, nothing is digested, and the action staggers shakily from line to line. The first run-through of *Hadrian* was at the end of the second week. By the end of the first act I was exhausted; then, as the longer second act proceeded, I felt uncertain that I would get to the end of the play. I was dizzy with fatigue. There were not sufficient reserves of energy inside me and I was genuinely frightened that, even with the cuts in the script, I had shouldered too great a load.

However, I kept these fears to myself. I was experienced enough to realize that I was forcing a performance out of myself mechanically, and that I hadn't yet absorbed the over-all intentions of the character.

The similarity of the play to working in a revue also struck me. I once ventured into this field with disastrous results – but at least I learnt the difficult technique of appearing in short sketches in rapid succession: being able to discard one character and situation, and present a new one – without any time for preparation – indeed sometimes scarcely any time for the necessary change of costume. *Hadrian* moved with this sort of rapidity; from a scene of vituperation to a scene of painful confession; from a wild scene of abandoned exhilaration to a tender scene of unspoken love. Finishing with one situation, hurriedly changing costume, and starting another in a different setting and in a completely different key. The character is so complex that he seemed at first to be a series of utterly different people, and there was no time to linger over the departing personality and present the next. I needed to find a magic word or phrase before each scene in order to effect the change of mood; something that would enable me to change gear without jolting the play and straining myself. But, at this stage of rehearsal, at the end of each scene I was too busy making mental notes of all the things that needed changing, re-rehearsing and rethinking, to be able to enter into the next situation with a clear mind and a definite objective.

I returned to the hotel feeling overwhelmed and dejected, convinced that this would be my last play, and pondering cosy thoughts of suicide. My sleep was spent in nightmares of public ineptitude and riotous confusion. The only comfort was in recognizing the symptoms from countless other unhappy rehearsals of other plays in other theatres; indeed recognizing the nightmares, the actor's nightmares of audiences jeering, of memory failure; ignorance not only of the dialogue but even of the play itself; not recognizing one's own make-up and costume; not finding the way from one's dressing-room to the stage; not even knowing the whereabouts of the theatre itself! (This nightmare actually occurred in reality during the Royal Shakespeare Company's tour of Eastern Europe. We were playing in a vast theatre in Warsaw. The dressing-rooms were up many flights of stairs. On the first night I had forgotten which floor was stage level – all directions were in Polish – and I listened helplessly to the play relayed on a loudspeaker as my cue got nearer and nearer and I ran along empty corridors searching for the stage. My entrance was breathless.)

After the first run-through we started working in detail again, and the second run-through was not until the Thursday of the third week – only five days before the opening. By this time I had managed to humanize the play, to understand it in my own terms, and to avoid the uncertain and fallible use of pure imagination. Although I had much in common with the personality of the character, his dreams were not my dreams, his antagonists were unreal, and his frustration and anger were foreign to me.

In order to make the play come fully alive I had to substitute the world of Hadrian for a world of my own, in which I could understand the environment, the friends, the enemies and the thwarted ambition. I learnt this trick of substitution from Vivian Matalon, who calls it making an 'As If'. In many of the plays in which one appears, the situations and the relationships are remote from one's own life, but in order to act the play fully, these situations and relationships must be understood. The only way to do this is to substitute parallel situations from one's own experience.

As far as *Hadrian* was concerned, I personally had no interest or even knowledge of the Catholic Faith or the Catholic Church. I had never met a Cardinal. I had no desire to be a priest. How could I make *Hadrian* come alive?

To go into great detail would probably reduce the whole task to absurdity. In general terms I substituted a world I knew very well – the world of the theatre. For the early scenes of frustration and anonymity, I recalled my own early days of unemployment and my early experience of living in small bed-sitters, when the ring of a telephone made one start with the anticipation of possible work; when a letter could possibly mean the fulfilment of one's hopes, and the act of unsealing the envelope might be the most dramatic moment of the day. I recalled the succession of disappointments; snubs from theatrical agents – snubs from the theatrical agent's secretaries; the necessity of overcoming one's jealousy of more fortunate colleagues; the fear that one's life would be wasted, and yet the desperate need to keep oneself in a state of mental and physical fitness in case the hoped-for opportunity suddenly occurred. It took Rolfe twenty years before – in his imagination – they came to ask him to enter the Church. In his fury at their neglect, he makes them beg before he will accept his life-long desire of the priesthood. I tried to imagine twenty years of unemployment; twenty years of un-answered letters and unsuccessful auditions. And then, sud-denly, as a result of this personal substitution, the gorgeous invective of the man came more easily to life.

The strain went out of the performance, and at the end of the second run-through I had a surge of energy and excitement that was almost bewildering in its intensity. Far from the fatigue and depression I had felt the first time, I now felt drunk with power and delight. It was impossible to return to the hotel and I went for a three-mile walk – often breaking into a run, and jumping in the air like a demented schoolboy. The long, tired bus queues of Birmingham workers looked on in astonishment as I passed by them – travelling in a state of virtual elevation down the Bristol Road. Actually, just over twenty years ago, I had worked in Birmingham at another repertory theatre and had often returned down this very road to my ghastly digs, feeling obscure and unhappy, sometimes doing work I did not respect, and dreading the loneliness of my bed-sitter. I went in search of the house – but it had been pulled down and the surrounding neighbourhood was almost unrecognizable. I continued my walk until I reached the Cathedral and stood listening to the noisy starlings. Then I had dinner and got drunk on some heavy red wine in order to dull my brain and get some sleep.

The fact is that for the first time I realized that I could play the part, and I also realized the splendour of the opportunity. That upsurge of energy after the second run-through is a clear indication of the link between mental confidence and physical well-being. That evening I was a super-man; but the next day I returned to earth with a heavy bump.

It is of course natural after a very successful rehearsal or performance to try to repeat it – instead of trying to re-create it. There is a world of difference. The memory of the previous performance lingers on. There is an echo of the inflexions, an impression of the effects created, the tensions achieved. And one stumbles into the error of an impersonation instead of a performance. The thoughts that gave birth to good acting are not there, and a reliance on remembering the result, without remembering the preparation that gave it birth, is an imperfect and inaccurate way of working – and gives way to a dead performance. The third and final run-through of *Hadrian* on that Friday was a dead performance.

In addition to this, I had the shock of discovering that I didn't really know my lines. On the Thursday I had winged my way through the play on a flight of emotional inspiration – leaving things out where it suited me, and transposing the dialogue when the right words evaded me. It was a great surprise to discover that I still had an enormous amount of work to do. Learning lines has never been a problem for me – indeed it has always been the least of my problems as an actor. Now I was humbled by the terror of 'drying-up' – as I had done at least twenty times during that last appalling run-through – quite apart from realizing that I could not rely on nightly inspiration to get me through the performance.

I returned to London that evening, and spent Saturday and Sunday working desperately hard, almost obscuring my script with notes written in various coloured pencils; reminders of my intentions, relationships and activities; reminders of technical problems; and warnings of lines not accurately learnt. I recorded the entire part three times on a tape-recorder, which at least solidified the actual dialogue, but which became a great menace in the subsequent repetition of the play in Birmingham, London and New York. I never quite forgot the memory of those recordings and a part of me was always trying to repeat the inflexions and timing made in the isolation of my study – without the actual impact of my fellow actors.

This lack of time was not the fault of the director, Peter Dews.

We were working with a new and untried script, and some rehearsal time was inevitably lost on textual problems. There was also a good deal of purely mechanical drilling to be done – with the processions of the Cardinals, the entrances of the Swiss Guards, and the funeral of Hadrian at the end of the play. Peter quite rightly spent a lot of time getting these things into immaculate order. Then there was the fact that nearly all the members of the company were playing in *As You Like It* or *Richard II* every evening, and were absent during their matinées on Wednesday and Saturday. Finally, in the middle of rehearsals, the actress playing Rosalind in *As You Like It* fell ill, and Peter had to cancel rehearsals of *Hadrian* in order to rehearse her replacement. None of this affected his extraordinary buoyancy and almost unfailing good humour. I will always be grateful for his consideration towards me during all three productions of the play – although, like most actors, I was secretly glad when the rehearsal period was over and I could be boss. Peter was always the star of his rehearsals.

The whole business of the actor-director relationship is a fascinating affair. Any good actor admits the necessity of a director; he is as necessary as a father in the upbringing of a child. But when the child has grown up – or when a performance nears completion – there is the inevitable resentment. Independence must be achieved, and the father figure is rejected. There comes the time when you must do it ALONE, and selfishly you imagine the character belongs solely to you. This is as necessary to a good leading performance as it is to the child who has become a man. You have absorbed the guidance, the advice, the taste, the invention, and then it must flow out of the brain and heart and muscle of yourself.

The chief difficulty in the actor-director relationship is usually that of communication. Nearly every actor and director has his own particular way of working, and each speaks his own particular language. The actor has to find out the director's way of speech – and often he then has to translate it into his own terms. Personally I find that I can very seldom take instant direction – except over simple matters – and act on it. I need to mull over the director's suggestions, to examine for myself the areas where he is unhappy, and work on the offending passages in my own way – usually arriving at the same result, but having reached it by my own understanding.

The variety of direction that one encounters is often bewildering. Some directors seem to be professional talkers and one silently prays for them to keep quiet; others are so reticent that the actor literally has to beg them for instruction. 'Is it all right?' one asks – needing confirmation that one isn't actually invisible. 'Yes!' they reply, looking astonished at the question. 'What's your worry?'

There is a well-known and well-loved director who can barely express himself at all. He will say, 'I think you should try to be a little more . . . er . . . you know. And in the scene where you say Goodbye, don't . . . er . . . quite so much. Would you like to do it again?' There is another very fine but very shy director whose rehearsals, once he has blocked the play, are entirely composed of run-throughs. At the end he will come forward with three notes written on the back of a small envelope, give one of them, then say apologetically, 'I don't think we'll bother with the other two. Let's run it again!' Then, after a drink in the pub at the end of the day, one gathers from oblique references to the progress of the play what work one should do. There are other directors whose notes take longer to give than the running time of the play itself. There is the blessedly specific director who will find you the right verbs, and there is the useless aesthete who will give the hazy instruction that 'it needs more . . . atmosphere' or 'it needs more . . . style'. There is the trendy university type who directs by asking questions, and the Continental visitor who expresses himself by mime and dancing. (When I played Mercutio in Zeffirelli's original production of *Romeo and Juliet* at the Old Vic, he danced the entire Queen Mab speech for me. I stood and watched, feeling square and stiff; hopelessly a son of Tunbridge Wells rather than Verona.) There are frightening directors who adopt a high moral tone and treat one as a potential criminal who is trying to sabotage their blue print for perfection, and there are directors for whom rehearsals are a tiresome interruption of a happy social occasion for drinking coffee and telling stories. There is the director who seems – depressingly – to be a much better actor than you yourself, and who cannot resist taking over a scene. There are directors who say 'You've lost it!' just when you think you've found it, and directors who brightly suggest you try to do a scene exactly as you think you have just done it. There is the director who works from constricting and copious notes made before rehearsals begin, and I once worked with a director who announced on the first day of rehearsal, 'Now we embark on a voyage of discovery' – which meant that he had done no work at all.

Peter Dews

None of these descriptions completely fits Peter Dews. He adores jokes and outrageous puns; indeed when he gives notes it frequently turns into a cabaret. He can work in the most extraordinary detail, giving an interpretation to almost every single word. He may then be completely uninterested in watching the finished result. He is, as I have already described, almost unfailingly good humoured, cajoling actors along with gentle hints and suggestions; but, occasionally, when his patience is completely exhausted, he quite unexpectedly explodes.

It happened only once at Birmingham, and happened fairly understandably during the first dress rehearsal.

The first dress rehearsal of any play – and in rep. it is quite often the only dress rehearsal because there is no time for another – is a very fraught occasion. It is usually the first time one has worked in the set – which is never quite finished, and there is hammering going on, and wet paint to be avoided, and often no door-handles or light-switches – and it is usually the first time one has worn the costumes – which are never entirely right, and your collar is too tight, and there is no pocket for your props, and you've forgotten to bring your braces. The director is exhausted from having spent the previous night lighting the play – and is impatient with actors who unexpectedly find themselves playing in the dark when they expected a blaze of light. 'We haven't finished it yet! Don't worry! You'll be seen! Get on with it!' The actor is in a state of turmoil because the position of furniture is slightly different, his costume is full of pins, nobody has noticed his subtle make-up, and he doesn't know where he'll do his quick change. His dressing-room is a hovel: there are no hooks, the mirror is cracked, and the cleaners have not had time to sweep out the previous owner's debris. Everybody is nervous with their own particular problems, and the director is on the receiving end of most of them. It is best to keep as quiet as possible, and certainly not the time to argue. The only sure way to get any attention is to burst into tears or to faint.

We got through the first act of *Hadrian* until the procession of the Cardinals, Papal Guards, Chamberlains and Acolytes. Then Peter decided to stop the rehearsal and inspect their costumes and make-up. The average age of the company was about twenty-two, and I think some of the Cardinals were actually still in their teens. A motley selection of spectacles and crepe-hair was handed out and some of the youngsters were advised to grey their hair with grease-paint or powder. A baby Cardinal demurred, and suddenly I heard a noise like the breaking of the sound barrier. 'GREY-UP!' Peter had exploded. The next minute he was his beaming self again and the rehearsal continued.

That was the Monday. The next day, Tuesday, 9 May, was the first performance of *Hadrian VII*. I remember absolutely nothing about it. In my diary I simply wrote that it 'went rather well'. After the performance there was a party for the cast in Peter's office and an agent friend of mine from New York, who was also a friend of the producer, Bill Freedman, told me confidentially that he was sorry, but in its present form, 'the play won't do . . .' I ate a dreadful 'He-Man-Grill' at a modest restaurant near the theatre and went to bed.

The next day, Wednesday, there were reviews in *The Times* and *Telegraph* and the *Guardian*. All of them were good for me, but there were qualifications about the play. Irving Wardle in *The Times* wrote: 'The hero's ascent from indigent obscurity to St Peter's chair is charted in a series of leapfrog jumps, paying off old scores on the way, and, if nothing else, the play proves Rolfe's corrosive dialogue to be brilliantly speakable. Alec McCowen caps his performance in *After the Rain* with another potent display of spiritual realpolitick . . .' and finished his review by writing, 'Relieved of its shaky superstructure and with some tightening up in the second act, the play would be well worth a London transfer.' Eric Shorter in the *Telegraph*, with the headline 'Dream Pope Holds Attention', wrote: '. . . If the play could somehow be compressed so that we get to Rome more quickly, the point of the adaptation would increase theatrically.' And Gareth Lloyd Evans in the *Guardian* wrote: 'It is, in effect, a no-play, given tremendous theatrical power by the intensity of its direction and playing.'

Wednesday was also a matinée day, and we played to two depressingly empty houses. There was no activity at the box-office, and already it seemed as if Birmingham was not going to be interested, and certainly – from the silence of the little audiences – not amused.

Then on the Thursday, because the company was still playing in repertory, I had a day off. As vividly as I remember the first day of rehearsal, I remember sitting on the terrace of the Albany Hotel, blinking in the May sunshine, and drinking Daquiris with Brian Cox – who was playing the impossible role of the villain, Jeremiah Sant. We had a few. Then I slept all afternoon and went to see Ken Dodd at the Birmingham Hippodrome in the evening. It was a gorgeous day.

The feeble response to the play from the public was, of course, deeply depressing to Peter Dews and me. Peter had the additional worry that the theatre had spent a great deal of money on the production and it looked as if, at the end of three weeks, they would be left with a pile of bills to pay for the expensive robes and uniforms. It is also depressing when a repertory company dares to put on a new play – which is a fairly rare occurrence – if their audience does not support them. The director is left with the unadventurous policy of producing popular classics or proven West End successes.

I found it very hard to forgive Birmingham for its lack of interest, but I was nevertheless exhilarated by the complexity of the role, and found each performance a challenging adventure. Gradually the man became more understandable and his behaviour became more and more natural to me.

As it turned out, the three weeks at Birmingham were only an initial work-out on the character, and we also learnt what went well in the play and what needed changing.

On the final Saturday the producers, Bill Freedman and Charles Kasher, came to the matinée to take a last look at their property. Also, unknown to me, Bernard Miles's General Manager, Ken Smalley, came up from London to see if *Hadrian* might be suitable for a future production at the Mermaid Theatre. I think that the cast outnumbered the audience, and I was convinced that this would be the end of *Hadrian VII*. Astonishingly, Bill and Charles decided to renew their option on the play and, also astonishingly, Ken Smalley decided to recommend it for the Mermaid. But there was, of course, no date for this, and we all knew there was much work to do on the script before we could embark on another production.

After the last performance, I said my goodbyes and packed up my belongings in the drab dressing-room – which had a mournful piece of information written on one of the walls to the effect that 'Ewen Solon wept here' – and wandered back to the hotel feeling very lonely and flat. I decided to go out again and search for the company; found most of them in a popular Chinese restaurant near the theatre, and we had a last, lively, wildly indigestible meal together.

The next day I got on one of those vague Sunday trains that wander through the countryside, and arrived at York in the late afternoon to take part in a Charity Concert for my favourite old repertory theatre. That night I found myself standing in the wings, where I had once been a humble assistant stage-manager, roaring with laughter at Frankie Howerd as he entertained the audience with deceptive effortless ease. By contrast it seemed such a pedestrian and boring occupation to be a straight actor.

'Wilt thou accept pontificality?' Rolfe is asked in *Hadrian*.

Personally, I'd much rather be a comic.

Interlude – London, New York

During the next three months I did a gramophone recording of *The Three Sisters*, an unlikely lunch-time recital of W. H. Auden's poetry in Westminster Abbey, and some broadcasting.

I have always adored working for the radio; for one thing you don't have to take off your clothes – and for another you don't have to learn your lines.

For me, Broadcasting House has always been a very glamorous place, associated in my mind with childhood memories of *Saturday Night Music Hall*, *Monday Night at Eight*, and Arthur Askey and Richard Murdoch in *Band Waggon*. It is also shaped like a womb, and once inside it I feel enormously safe. Of course the original oval building now has a vast modern extension attached to it, but I find it still echoes with the thirties. Stuart Hibberd informing the nation that, 'The King's life is drawing peacefully towards its close'; the announcer who delighted us all with 'The whole damn fleet's lit up!' – and the thrill of discovering who was going to be 'In Town Tonight'. As a child I was almost ill with excitement when they broadcast a short extract of a sound track with Garbo's voice on it. The sensation of hearing her voice – HER VOICE! – in our little living-room was beyond belief; and I went around in circles, punching cushions and looking at the well-known surroundings with new eyes. The world seemed so much smaller – and anything seemed possible. Garbo was here! Well, if Garbo was here – where mightn't *I* go!

Perhaps for each generation there can only be one invention that really stuns the imagination. The brain will not take any more. Splitting the atom and television are things which I have never absorbed. Walking on the moon is pure Walt Disney. The telephone and the gramophone were already part of my childhood. But the radio still astonishes me, and the thought that my voice might be heard in anyone's living-room – or on anyone's car radio – is a perpetual source of wonder to me. I remember during my first live broadcast that I was unable to concentrate as thoughts of possible listeners flashed through my mind. Was Clement Attlee switched on? Was Auntie Olive listening? Do they have a set at Buckingham Palace? If I stumble over my lines, will it be the end of my career? Does the BBC realize how easy it would be for me to leave the script and swear or belch or incite a revolution? It still seems to me the most powerful of all the media, and I feel an enormous sense of importance when I face a microphone.

The contrast of this excitement with the relaxed attitudes of the regular broadcasters is an additional delight. Experienced members of the BBC Repertory Company will sit around during rehearsals, and even during the actual recording, doing their crosswords, knitting, and occasionally falling asleep. But when the cue comes, they are there at the mike, sometimes speaking in wild accents, sometimes imitating dogs or babies, sometimes weeping, sometimes laughing, and sometimes making passionate love by kissing the backs of their hands and breathing deeply, before they return to their crosswords and knitting – or to the script of their next assignment. And then, at the end of the day, they emerge into the rush-hour, anonymous amongst the conventional workers of Oxford Street, who will never guess that the stranger sitting beside them, in bus or tube, is the owner of a voice they know intimately.

I love Broadcasting House – the coffee breaks; the canteen with the scones, the raspberry jam and the yoghurt; the complaints about the lifts; the imperfect air-conditioning; and the generous number of lavatories on every floor. By contrast, working conditions in the theatre, in television, and in film studios, are nothing like as cosy, and the additional embrace of that womb-like building gives an illusion of permanence and security.

On the Royal Shakespeare tour of *King Lear*, during the storm scene – which we both hated doing – Paul Scofield and I devised a little game. The clothes were uncomfortable; the strain on the voice against the thunder claps was painful; the miming of imaginary wind and rain was tiring and felt ridiculous; and we both wished we were safely back in England doing a broadcast. At a particularly noisy clap of thunder we would murmur in each other's ear the name of a member of the BBC Repertory

34

Company – Marjorie Westbury, Norman Shelley or Rolf Lefebvre – which somehow gave us the strength to continue our battle against the elements.

During the summer of 1967 I did four broadcasts – including the title role in Chekov's uproarious tragedy *Ivanov*, and Thomas Mendip in *The Lady's not for Burning*.

Also during this time there was a meeting with the *Hadrian* gang – Freedman, Kasher, Dews and Luke – about the changes to be made in the script. And I had lunch with Mr and Mrs Bernard Miles at the Mermaid Theatre, who looked a bit glum when I told them the size of the cast. A future production of Peter Luke's play still seemed very remote to me.

I had a splendid holiday driving through France; then I flew to New York to do the American production of *After the Rain*.

I was met at Kennedy Airport by Vivian Matalon. He had already been there for a couple of weeks auditioning American actors. We drove to the Meurice Hotel on 58th Street, which was to become my second home during my three visits to New York in the next four years.

In the sitting-room of my suite, standing in front of the huge gaping unused fireplace – complete with brass tongs and a poker – stood a large vase of flowers from the producer, Helen Jacobson. And on the polished table was a bottle of whisky from my agent, Janet Roberts. Soon I would get to know the friendly hotel staff: the talkative doorman called Donald who, like most Americans, called me Mr McGowan – McCowen seems to be very difficult to pronounce; Dolores, the equally talkative and affectionate switchboard girl; and the rota of elevator men who took an almost embarrassing interest in the fortunes of the play.

Vivian drove me down to see the display for *After the Rain* outside the Golden Theatre, where he had recently got them to correct the spelling of my name, and told me of his progress with the casting.

The next day I read with several actors for the eight parts to be acted by Americans. Their Equity had allowed only four British actors to work in New York and, since the play was very much an ensemble production, it was important that we should not clash. Because of the dreadful lack of employment in New York, even leading American actors expect to audition – and are usually astonished by the courtesy shown them by English directors.

Donald, the doorman at the Meurice

I had lunch at New York's fashionable theatrical restaurant, Sardi's, with Helen Jacobson, who arranged to have one of the prestige tables – which are placed in a draught near the entrance where everyone coming in or leaving can see you, and where you are jostled by table hoppers and waiters who have not got enough room to move. It is imperative to sit at one of these tables if you wish to be respected in the tiny theatrical village of New York. If you are in a hit you are seated in this area automatically, but when business starts to slip – or if the show is a flop – you may find yourself being placed further into the restaurant; where it is a good deal more comfortable, but nobody gives a damn.

After the readings at the theatre we had supper at Sardi's and the following day my agent took me to lunch there, by which time I had a stiff neck from the draught and decided that I didn't want to be a fashionable Broadway star.

We had a busy week casting, being photographed, seeing old friends, and looking for new places to eat. Then, before starting rehearsals, Vivian took me to spend a weekend with his friend and teacher Sanford Meisner – who had taken a summer house at Amaganset, Long Island. Sandy Meisner is one of the great men of the American theatre and the enormous debt owed to him by the countless American actors, whom he has taught cannot be sufficiently acknowledged. In his office at the Neighbourhood Playhouse is a quotation from Goethe: 'I wish the stage were as narrow as the wire of a tightrope dancer, so that no incompetent would dare step upon it.' His judgement upon a performance is hypercritical, and his praise is worth more than anyone else I know.

But that weekend we were all relaxing, and Sandy introduced me to a superb new drink, the bullshot; made with vodka, beef bouillon, tabasco and fresh lime. I will never forget that first taste in the hot sun on the lawn at Amaganset – followed by barbecued hamburgers and a sleep in the shade.

Vivian and I were very excited to be doing *After the Rain* in America. Although I had played in New York with the Royal Shakespeare Company, and had also played small parts with Laurence Olivier and Vivien Leigh in their 1952 season at the Ziegfeld Theatre in *Antony and Cleopatra* and *Caesar and Cleopatra*, this was the first time that I had starred on Broadway in a contemporary play. And for Vivian, it was a triumphant return to the city where he had struggled as a young actor. We were both determined not to become embroiled in the usual hysteria which seems to beset any new Broadway show. The difference between doing a play in America and England is very great. The dramas which arise in America, the conferences, the sackings, the traditional publicity stunts and the vast amount of advertising, the tensions caused by the tremendous potential economic gains or losses, make an English production seem like the relative peace of amateur night in the Village Hall. It was a great comfort that we were not first going to tour the play, as this would remove the arguments and fears aroused by the reviews of out-of-town critics.

However, we were not quite able to sustain our resolution. After four weeks' rehearsal in a temperature of eighty degrees; after some bad-tempered conferences about re-writes; after too many late nights in a city where it is difficult to go to sleep; after we had all been disciplined once too often by a zealous stage-manager about our slightest departure from the text; after the noise in the theatre of the air-conditioning plant, which had made us inaudible during the first two previews; after discovering that the next door hotel always emptied its garbage into dustbins during one of the quietest scenes of the play; after discovering that we could plainly hear the orchestra and chorus of *Fiddler on the Roof* who were playing in one of the theatres which backed on to us; after tracing other sounds of voices and music to the stage-hands' television set under the stage – and finding that they were extremely reluctant to switch off; and, finally, after discovering that our first night clashed with the first New York appearance of Marlene Dietrich who was getting all the publicity; I was tired, tetchy and nervous. In fact during a particularly trying rehearsal I did something which I have never done before: I walked out. This cleared the air a great deal and good humour returned. That evening, in front of the entire company, I apologized to Vivian. Vivian apologized to me. Helen Jacobson apologized to everybody. Then Vivian and I went out and drank bourbon and ate spare ribs. At least New York was living up to its reputation.

After a week of previews, we opened. After the show Helen gave a party in the Belasco Room at Sardi's. There was an orchestra, enormous amounts of food and drink, and a visit from my theatre-mad American cousins from Cleveland who had flown to New York especially for the occasion. And Elaine Stritch sang a song.

Personally, I prefer the English way of reading the notices of a new play on the following day. The excitement of a first night is quite enough without having the whole thing reviewed almost immediately afterwards. I would rather eat and drink and relax with friends. But in New York, the first reviews may start coming out within an hour of the curtain coming down. These are the reviews by the television critics. Each channel has its own critic, and at these first-night parties in Sardi's, television sets are turned on, either in the restaurant or in the offices upstairs, and one's merriment may suddenly be changed to tears; food may become indigestible; and a celebration can turn into a wake. On one occasion, when I was not involved except as an onlooker, I saw the entire cast of a musical quietly disappear from the restaurant as it became clear with each successive bad TV notice that their show would not last the week. Waiters can turn surly and the generous hosting producer is often the first to leave. However, if these early TV notices are good – or even reasonable – the party may continue until the great moment of the arrival of the *New York Times* – usually at about 1 a.m. This is the really serious event. This is the notice which really counts, and on this notice will depend the immediate future of all involved in the production.

These first-night parties in New York always remind me of a British Election night. The early notices give an indication of the way things are going. I always want to say, 'It looks as if we are going to get in,' when I am told these are favourable. But then the *New York Times* – in one fell swoop – can give the final result without waiting for any other opinion.

We seemed to be doing quite well with *After the Rain* when I arrived, a little late, at the party. 'We got two favourable,' I was informed by one of the American members of the cast. I tried to forget the play and concentrated on food, friends and my American cousins from Cleveland. Then copies of the *New York Times* arrived, silence was called for, and Helen Jacobson asked her teenaged daughter to read the entire notice aloud to the assembly, which was a fairly daring move. Luckily it was a very good notice by English standards. Clive Barnes wrote that: 'Mr Bowen's play extends the mind – not that far but far enough for us to feel the stretch, and a sensible man will exult in wild moderation.' He also wrote of 'the authoritative direction of Vivian Matalon', and that, 'outstanding was Alec McCowen as the leader, bespectacled, tersely fanatic and with a voice like a shark in an aquarium'. It seemed as if we had succeeded and the party continued happily.

We were over-optimistic. The *New York Times*'s headline, 'Play that extends the mind', was not the most attractive carrot for Broadway audiences in search of an evening's escapism. And even if we had not already been somewhat eclipsed by Marlene Dietrich's dazzling opening on the same night, the following week Tom Stoppard's play, *Rosencrantz and Guildenstern*, arrived to unqualified 'raves'. Broadway can usually only absorb one intellectual product a year, and for the 1967–68 season they chose *Rosencrantz and Guildenstern*.

At the Golden Theatre I saw those empty rows of seats again. Soon the company started to whisper about lack of publicity, and at the Meurice Hotel, the elevator men – all of whom seemed to read *Variety* – began to treat me as someone close to a bereavement.

There is an inevitable lowering of morale in a company on these occasions. Sometimes this can lead to a slack performance of the play. Sometimes it can lead to intense over-acting as if to compensate for the lack of reaction. With *After the Rain* – in which we were supposed to be playing hypnotized criminals – there were one or two regrettable outbreaks of corpsing – or giggling – and some of us were unable to look each other in the eye. The worst instance occurred when one of the cast farted quite loudly during a performance. Rising hysteria might have been suppressed until it was realized that my next line was, 'There came a great wind over the surface of the waters.'

These outbreaks of giggling are followed by dreadful remorse and solemn promises to the stage-manager that they will never happen again. It is difficult to explain this childish behaviour to anyone outside the theatre; the slightest deviation from the text can cause an actor to choke with laughter, and small unforeseen accidents can lead to hysteria. (When playing Hamlet, I inadvertently spat in Gertrude's eye from a great distance and saw her flinch. Unable to continue, I buried my head in the folds of her dressing-gown for a full minute, and eventually emerged with streaming eyes; a theatrical moment that was greatly praised by a member of the audience afterwards.)

But the fate of *After the Rain* in New York was very sad for all of us, and these outbursts of hilarity were actually manifestations of our great disappointment.

Of course there were the enthusiasts who came backstage and said '*I* liked it!' as if they had made a personal discovery in the face of opposition; there were others – expecting only to 'extend their minds' – who exclaimed, 'But it's very *funny*!' – as if we had purposely kept this fact a secret. There were those who said, 'It should have played off-Broadway,' and there was one admirer who told me helpfully: 'Of course what it needs is a *real* star.'

The stage door of the Golden Theatre is down an alley where three theatres back on to each other. One night after the show a small boy came into my dressing-room and asked for Lauren Bacall's autograph. She was playing next door. Perhaps she should have done *After the Rain*.

We dwindled on for eight weeks – which was the same length

of time the play had run in London – then Helen Jacobson decided to close it.

After a trip to Philadelphia to see my favourite Cezanne, and a trip to Cleveland to see my American cousins, I returned to England feeling very sorry for myself. *The Cavern* had failed. *After the Rain* had failed. *Hadrian VII* had failed. I longed to be back in the comparative security of one of the Classical Companies. The Commercial Theatre seemed too tough for me.

The next three months were a very low ebb.

I read an announcement in a newspaper of the Mermaid Theatre's plans for 1968 which made no mention of *Hadrian VII*, and indeed even if a production of *Hadrian* was eventually set up, I could see no reason why the play would succeed with the public in London any more than it had in Birmingham.

My bank balance was low, my morale was even lower and, as if to punish myself further, in the freezing January gloom I went off to a Health Farm and starved for a couple of weeks.

After a year of screaming my guts out in three successive productions in gapingly empty theatres, I thought it was time to give the theatre a rest. I did a gramophone recording of *The Importance of Being Earnest*, a TV commentary on pot-holing – in which I had to be replaced by a more gravel-voiced actor – and from time to time returned to the comforting womb of Broadcasting House for more scones, raspberry jam and yoghurt.

Then . . .

London

In the middle of February 1968 Larry Dalzell rang to say that there was a definite date for *Hadrian* at the Mermaid, and that rehearsals would start in four weeks' time.

I roused myself from despondency and determined to have another bash at the theatre. In fact I was more determined than ever before. If I couldn't pull it off with a part as great and glorious as Hadrian, I might as well give up. Luckily, Peter Dews, who had also had his share of bad luck, was equally determined, and we both realized how lucky we were to be given a second chance.

It is true that every time you do a new play, a new film, a new television appearance, you wish for its and your own success. And it is true that I was – and always had been – a fiendishly ambitious young actor. But since arriving at the age of forty without achieving young dreams of stardom, I was more inclined to act to please myself rather than audiences or critics, and to do work that I respected, rather than do work that would bring accolades or big financial gains. The realization with the passing years that one is involved in a somewhat ridiculous profession, an extension of the childhood games of 'Dressing up' and 'Let's pretend', gradually weighs upon actors approaching middle age – often leading to the brusque and touchy temperaments of many character-men. But a sense of adventure always remains, even if it is buried deep down; and the extraordinary chancy element of the profession lends it excitement. At one moment there may be unemployment with no prospects of work; then a phone call or an interview may lead to a film in the South Seas, a tour of Welsh mining towns, an operation in a television hospital, or a play at the Haymarket.

My sense of adventure was not buried very deep, and I vowed to have one more attempt to throw my cap over the moon. Many years ago a fortune-teller in Liverpool had read my palm. She told me that I belonged to an artistic profession, that I had much talent, but that I would never throw my cap over the moon

– neither as an actor nor as a human being. This had somewhat dampened my spirits at the time, and indeed whenever a great potential opportunity occurred I was always haunted by her prophecy.

This time I would prove her wrong.

In the beginning is the word.

Nowadays it is impossible for an actor to create a success without a good script. It seems as if in Irving's day audiences were less critical, and actors could sometimes entertain with crude pieces of terror or hysteria, comic business and hypnotism. But today an actor must acknowledge that the playwright is his master, and that his job as an actor is to interpret his master's voice. (This loyalty is not always so binding to film scripts which, strangely, do not attain a comparable standard – despite the money spent on them.)

While I was away, much work had been done on the script of *Hadrian* – notably by Peter Dews. Peter Luke had good-naturedly given him permission to make further cuts, and they had also tried to strengthen the motives of the villain of the piece, Jeremiah Sant.

The original script was now cut from 104 to 77 pages, and I was delighted. It is very foolish to imagine that a big part is necessarily a good one – or to think that the bigger the role the better it is. Often one sees a fine performance by a leading actor that just goes on too long. There is great danger in tiring an audience with needless repetition and too many climaxes. There is danger for an actor that an audience sees too much of his face and hears too much of his voice. A good leading actor is not only behaving unselfishly when he gives away scenes to supporting actors, he is also behaving sensibly – even cunningly. He has plenty of opportunities to make his presence felt, and it can be just as fascinating to watch someone listen superbly as it is to watch and hear them tear a passion to tatters.

I spent a couple of days with Peter Dews and his wife at their home in Whitstable, working on the script and discussing the future production. I was particularly pleased that two rather embarrassing prayers had been removed; prayers where I had been left alone on stage in a single spotlight – and according to Peter had appeared to sound and look like a close relative of St Joan. I knew that I had been indulging myself in these scenes –

but alone on stage, in a spotlight, it is difficult to resist the temptation.

Often in the past, people – friends and colleagues – had accused me of being too retiring, unassertive and over-modest. If I wished to succeed as an actor – or to attain stardom – they said that I should try to sell myself more, push myself forward and get into the spotlight. Once in the spotlight on stage I had always been a natural ham; but off-stage it had never appealed to me.

This is not due to any genuine modesty in my nature. In fact the explanation of my so-called retiring personality is the reverse of its appearance. Such has been my conceit that I always expected recognition, fame and applause, without having to sell myself, without having to push or resort to publicity and salesmanship. Perhaps the childhood awe of Garbo had impressed me so deeply – the legend of the star who refused all requests for interviews and publicity, and by these tactics had become even more fascinating than her contemporaries – that I thought myself equally magnetic. In any case for years I had waited for a breathless world to discover me, without raising a finger to help them in the search.

It is equally true that I dislike being stared at off-stage, and enjoy the luxury of leading an anonymous existence. It is also true that the attraction of great fame and wealth, and all that goes with them, has never been strong. In fact, ideally, it would be pleasant to have success without notoriety, and adulation without the curiosity and pestering attention of fans and admirers. Also, from a practical point of view, it seems to me important for an actor to lead a normal everyday life – with all the frustrations and indignities that go with it – if he is to go on portraying recognizable human beings with any success.

Now, with the approaching production of *Hadrian*, and the opportunity given to me of playing a great virtuoso role in London, I decided to think again. My retiring, modest-violet act had not been much of a success in the past. I had a drawer full of good notices from critics, gathered over many years, but outside the profession I was virtually unknown. I was forty-two, not much to look at, already over-shadowed professionally by many fine actors much younger than myself. Damn it! I decided to get a press-agent.

This idea seemed like the most daring act of my professional life. It also seemed to the Garbo deep down inside me like a dreadful sell-out!

Twenty years before, when I first came to try my luck in London, I had met a young press-agent called Eric Braun. Eric was just beginning to break into the theatrical scene, and he worked in a small office in Earls Court. I was out of work and living, practically on charity, with a dear married couple, Lala Lloyd and David Raven, whom I had met when we were all in rep. together at Scarborough. This was a very bleak time professionally, when I was reduced to being a poodle-sitter for David and Lala; they were busily engaged during the day and evening, and needed someone to feed and walk the dog. The dog was called Shandy, and she was very fond of me except when the phone rang. Then, as I dashed to pick up the receiver hoping for offers of work, Shandy would turn into a savage, bite my ankles and do anything in her power to prevent me reaching the telephone. It was a difficult relationship.

It happened also at this time that Eric Braun needed someone to answer his phone and take messages whenever he had to go out on business, and he asked me if I would do this for a small fee. I gladly accepted the offer.

Remembering this now, I asked Eric if he would be my press-agent for the next few weeks, to cover the rehearsals and opening of *Hadrian*.

Since the Mermaid had got a very keen young lady called Caroline Rockman working for them in the same capacity to represent the theatre, I felt that this time there could be no reproaches about lack of publicity – even if there were those ghastly rows of empty seats again.

God knows if any of this made the slightest bit of difference to the subsequent success of *Hadrian*, but at least I saw several references to the forthcoming production in various papers and magazines, and a certain amount of curiosity seemed to be aroused.

There was for instance the wild-looking young man standing next to me in a crowded underground train who noticed a copy of the play I was carrying. 'I'll be coming to the Mermaid,' he said in a threatening tone of voice. 'Do you like the theatre?' I asked. 'No,' he growled, 'but I dig *Corvo*, so you'd better be good!' I got off the train at the next station in a panic. The Corvines were obviously alerted.

Meanwhile Peter Dews was trying to cast the play – with great difficulty. At Birmingham the many character parts had been played by very young actors wearing heavy make-up. It would be a great help to have these parts played by actors of the right age and weight. But the Mermaid Theatre could not pay West End salaries, and it was proving difficult to tempt character men away from their better-paid work in films and TV. Young actors are used to working for a pittance, but older actors often have homes and families to support, quite apart from expecting proper remuneration for their longer experience. There was the additional drawback that the role of Hadrian was so huge and meaty that the supporting parts tended to seem puny by comparison. However, the quality of the actors playing these parts was vitally important to the success of the play.

I was delighted when my old friend Alan MacNaughtan agreed to play Dr Talacryn, Bishop of Caerleon. Alan had been in *After the Rain* and was used to hearing my confessions. He would now hear Rolfe's in *Hadrian* for many months to come.

Margaret Courtenay, Peggy Aitchison, Mary Gauntlet and Patrick McAlinney were other old friends in the company, which also included Otto Diamant, Brian Tully, Vivian Mackerell and Patrick Marley. But a couple of important parts remained uncast, which was very worrying.

Shortly before rehearsals started, Bill Freedman took me down to look at the Mermaid stage and I saw the first billboard outside the theatre advertising the coming production. My name was printed in such large letters that I blushed – as if someone had guessed my secret. Bill was delighted by my reaction. He is a quietly clever man, and he remained friendly and reassuring throughout the London and New York productions, always addressing me as 'Holiness' – 'May I leave my coat in your dressing-room, Holiness?' 'Coming for a drink, Holiness?' – and cannily making me feel important.

However, after the thrill of seeing my name in enormous letters, and having pleasurable intimations that I actually existed, my eye caught the announcement that the play was due to run for a six-week season. My heart sank. Four weeks of empty houses would be just bearable. Six weeks was too much. I pleaded with Bill to change the run to four weeks and then extend it if, by any chance, we did good business. Bill told me not to be so faint-hearted and to 'think big'. I tried to 'think big' but it was no use. I was out of practice. We seemed to be laying ourselves open for a spectacular flop – which would only interest a small number of Fr Rolfe's admirers, and which would surely be completely ignored by that elusive body, the theatre-going public.

With the Mermaid poster of *Hadrian VII*

Rehearsals started without a full cast, but eventually we were joined by Donald Eccles and Brian Coburn in the important roles of Dr Courtleigh, Cardinal-Archbishop of Pimlico, and Cardinal Ragna respectively.

I loved working on the large Mermaid Theatre stage, and being able to use the entire theatre as the setting for the Vatican. It often happens that even with a good play, a good cast and a good production, a play can be jeopardized by the actual theatre where it is housed. A modern setting will seem wrong in one of the ornate Edwardian theatres. An intimate drama gets lost in too large an auditorium. Attempts to act as if on an open stage behind a stubborn proscenium arch look obvious and contrived. But the Mermaid Theatre was absolutely right for Peter Dews's staging and Tim Goodchild's clever setting of *Hadrian*. The theatre might have been designed expressly for the play.

Rehearsals were uneventful; my only problem was to suppress impatience while the new cast learnt their lines, and to keep a brake on myself until they were at performance level. I longed to run the play, to get into costume, and to practise the very quick changes. Apart from these quick changes, with the new cuts I was now on stage for the whole of Act One and, after a short rest following the interval, for practically the whole of Act Two. It was vital to have no worries other than acting the play. I knew it was up to me to 'make the play happen'. I had to set the pace and drive it along.

At the first dress rehearsal, genial Peter Dews had one of his short outbursts, which startled an unsuspecting company. As he was drilling an unlikely selection of Swiss Guards, I heard the breaking of the sound barrier once again when he yelled, 'KEEP IN STEP!' After that, they did.

I was vastly relieved when I met my dresser, Ian Young, and discovered that not only was he superbly good at his job, but that he was very pleasant company in the dressing-room. The actor-dresser relationship is very delicate, and can only be understood by people in the profession. As well as doing his job, a good dresser must know when to talk and when to keep silent; when to appear and when to vanish. Ian Young had perfect timing.

There were three previews: the first was given to an audience mostly consisting of friends of the cast. We were all very nervous, and I had no idea how this strange play was going to be received by sophisticated London. At the moment when Rolfe is asked 'Wilt thou accept pontificality?' I paused for a very long time, looking in bewilderment at the Cardinals kneeling all around me. The question 'Wilt thou accept pontificality?' was asked again. I paused again. Then a shrill voice from a male member of the audience yelled out impatiently: 'Go on, girl! Take it!' The entire cast shuddered with laughter and I turned cold. At least audiences in Birmingham had been quiet, deathly quiet. Were we to be barracked in London?

All first nights are the same. I cannot remember any of them. They all merge into one.

A first night, of course, includes the day that leads up to the performance, and the whole chaos that goes on after it.

It is a day of ridiculous contradictions. The intention of everyone concerned in the production is to keep cool, calm and collected. But the behaviour of everyone concerned in the production usually creates an atmosphere of nervousness – bordering on insanity. 'It's just another show,' we tell each other falsely. And 'after all, critics are only human beings' we remind ourselves doubtfully. And 'I know you'll be marvellous' we say to colleagues – as if we had seen no previous signs of any talent whatsoever.

I get up in the morning and go through the everyday routines of bathing, shaving, dressing, drinking coffee – as if for the very last time. It is impossible to imagine the existence of tomorrow.

If I have been given the day off and I perhaps do some shopping for first-night cards and presents, a sudden twinge of fatigue will frighten me into believing that I have already used up the evening's strength. And the casual behaviour of shopkeepers, taxi-drivers and the general populace seems heartless and cruel as I nurse my private terror of the exposure to come.

If I stay at home I might lie down and try to rest – soon discovering that not only am I holding my breath, but my body is suspended one inch above the bed.

I get up and play a noisy gramophone record – Judy Garland or Sibelius – until I fear that I'm being emotionally drained and hurriedly switch off.

Then there is the awful conflict in one's mind, 'To pray or not to pray' . . . 'If it's an absolute disaster I'll look back to this moment and realize I should have asked God's help,' Or, 'Won't God admire me more if I achieve success without troubling Him?' Or, 'After all, I don't pray on ordinary days – mightn't it be hypocritical for me to pray today?' And, 'Who the hell do you think you are, anyway?' And, 'Beethoven's motto was "Man, help thyself!"' Etc., etc.

Finally, when I leave home to go to the theatre, I often say goodbye to my image in the mirror – as if the horror of the evening may actually change my appearance beyond recognition.

Most directors call the company in to the theatre for a

49

rehearsal in the afternoon – simply to give everyone something to do. 'We won't rehearse properly,' they say. 'Just run through some of the lines.' 'Don't strain your voice or tire yourselves.'

So you rehearse – improperly – without straining your voice or tiring yourselves, and immediately start to dry up and wonder whether you've forgotten the whole play.

Your dressing-room is full of telegrams from friends, and cards and little gifts from the company. You realize guiltily that you've forgotten several people in the cast – and *always* the designer.

At the end of the rehearsal the director thanks the actors, wishes everybody luck, and suddenly finds himself an unwanted man. The cast may go out to have a sandwich or an egg to keep their strength up. Then, much too early, you go to your dressing-room to get ready.

Soon there are little taps on the door and people wish you luck – as if they are saying goodbye for the last time. Worst of all are the producers, who are usually more nervous than the actors, since they have nothing to do but sit out front and watch. You try to soothe them, and wish they'd go away. Often the stage-management give you helpful last-minute tidbits of information such as 'The paint's still wet on the mantelpiece', or 'We've lost the newspaper you read in Act Two', and nearly always 'I'm sorry but that door's still sticking'.

You touch up your make-up for the tenth time – and then realize you look like a silent film star and rub it all off again.

They call the five minutes and add the information that the curtain will go up ten minutes late – so you have at least another fifteen minutes to kill.

You resist the temptation to go down to the stage, and start to pester the other members of the cast by knocking at their doors and wishing *them* luck. 'Good luck, darling! Enjoy it!' 'Have a ball!' 'Soon be over now!' 'Oh, you're wearing a different make-up! Yes, it's much better!' (Thank God I saw it before she came on!)

You return to your room and check your quick changes, and look at the script to find the first thing you ever wrote in it.

The first thing I wrote in the script of *Hadrian VII* was, 'A frightened man.' Yes, that's me all right!

I look at my mirror which is covered with private instructions written in capital letters with greasepaint. 'D.B.F.' – which

With mirror instructions

means, 'Don't Be Funny!' 'D.P.' – meaning, 'Don't Push!' 'R.R.' – 'Remember Relationships!' 'B.A.G.P.' – 'Be A Good Pope!' – and there are also warnings to remember personal props such as rings and cigarettes and matches.

I wonder if I have enough drinks and glasses for visitors after the show.

I wonder if anyone will come round after the show.

I wonder if I'll still be alive after the show.

I wonder – 'Beginners, please!'

Mrs Siddons described herself before a first night as being in a state of 'desperate tranquillity'.

Edith Evans, on being wished good luck before a performance replied, 'I don't need luck. I need application.'

I think you need both.

Because there is no curtain at the Mermaid Theatre, before the play started I used to sit on the stage in the dark in my little room – which was built on a revolving truck – and listen to the audience chattering. When everyone was in, the stage-manager gave the cue to dim the house-lights, and two young stage-hands, dressed in black habits like monks, used to push the revolving truck round. The lights came up to discover me sitting in my chair writing my book, until the landlady, Mrs Crowe, played by Margaret Courtenay, knocked at the door.

'Mr Rolfe! Mr Rolfe!'

'Tickle your arse with a feather!'

'What's that?'

'Particularly nasty weather!'

And we were off!

At the end of the play the audience cheered, and I went happily back to my dressing-room. Cheers on a first night are exhilarating to hear, although they are no guarantee of good notices the following morning. One may quite easily read that 'the audience were fooled into thinking they had seen entertainment of great quality' or 'there were cheers of sympathy for the cast at the end of the performance as I fled up the aisle'. But at least for the actors and all concerned in the production cheering is preferable to booing, and we could postpone our reactions to the reviews until the following day.

Backstage visitors were enthusiastic: Peter Dews, Bernard Miles and the producers were delighted. The only member of the team who was missing was Peter Luke. He had moved with his family to Spain, and the production company wouldn't pay the plane fare for him to see the opening of his play. After entertaining many people in my dressing-room I went off to have a huge Chinese meal at the Lotus House in Edgware Road with a group of friends and my sister, who had come up from Devon.

The following morning, Friday, my sister asked if I had ordered the papers for us to read the notices. I hadn't. She volunteered to go out and get them. I was reluctant and said that it would be a pity to spoil the day. Then a friend rang up in great excitement to say that he had read them all and they were marvellous. 'This is a theatrical experience not to be missed.' 'Alec McCowen exploded into a star of the first magnitude last night.' 'The most interesting play to be seen in London.' 'A performance that will be talked about for years.' 'Acting worth going miles to see.' 'Fascinating', 'enthralling', 'masterly', and so on.

The Mermaid was nearly full for the performances on Friday and Saturday – and I thought we would manage the six-week season. But I feared, as sometimes happens, the important Sunday reviews would be less enthusiastic.

It happens that the offices of the *Observer* are just across the road from the Mermaid Theatre. In order to make their great processional entrance through the auditorium, the Cardinals had to go out of the stage door, along the street and round to the front of house. On their journey during the Saturday matinée they collected early editions of the *Observer* and hid them under their robes. After electing me to be the Successor of St Peter – which was followed by the interval – they whipped out their copies of the *Observer* and gave me Ronald Bryden's notice to read.

The headline was 'Birth of a New Star'.

This notice and Harold Hobson's review in *The Sunday Times* – 'this splendid, colourful, recklessly melodramatic and vituperatively brilliant drama' – clinched the success of the play. On Monday night the house was full, and the future bookings were already tremendous.

I was interviewed by the press with headlines like 'Hadrian reflects on his triumph', 'From fool to father figure', and 'Fairy-tale Hadrian'. I was photographed by Lord Snowdon and Cecil Beaton. I was interviewed on the radio in Art's Magazine Programmes, *Woman's Hour* and Late Night Record shows.

Hadrian VII by Cecil Beaton

There was a special television programme devoted to my career. And, best of all, there were many letters from leading actors sending congratulations on my success.

It was obvious from the fantastic queues at the box-office that we could run the play indefinitely. There were conferences about transferring to a bigger West End theatre, but very wisely the producers decided to leave the play at the Mermaid for the time being and, with the agreement of Bernard Miles who cancelled his immediate plans for future Mermaid productions, we settled down to an indefinite run.

It was an astonishing summer. The success of the play seemed to grow greater every week. Lines of people waited outside the theatre for returned tickets. All of us in the company were besieged by friends and acquaintances hoping for seats. My telephone rang constantly with people saying, 'I know this is a terrible imposition but . . .' 'We've been to the box-office and they say they can't do anything till August.' '. . . and anyway why I'm *really* ringing you is to ask . . .', etc., etc.

Soon the play was ecstatically reviewed by American critics, and the enormous number of American tourists in London

54

found it impossible to go home without seeing *Hadrian*. It ranked with the Changing of the Guard and Westminster Abbey in their list of priorities.

Publicity mounted with the visits of Royalty. Princess Margaret came to see it twice. (She told me how pleased everyone had been when the Mermaid was built ten years previously. 'But,' she asked, 'isn't it time they finished it?')

My little dressing-room by the river was often full of celebrities, and sometimes Bernard Miles would entertain us afterwards in the Mermaid Restaurant.

In my dressing-room after the performance with friends

Olivier, Gielgud and Redgrave came to the play. There was an hilarious supper with Noël Coward, whose sophisticated theatrical stories contrasted superbly with Bernard's bucolic style. There was Carol Channing, who brought her own photographer but refused to take off her dark glasses because she'd lost one of her eyelashes. Prince Rainier and Princess Grace asked me to do a performance in Monaco. There was the occasion when my dresser Ian Young announced: 'There's a Mr Bing Crosby to see you,' and I said, 'Oh don't be ridiculous!' –

just as the well-known owner of the hat, pipe and blazer strolled into my room. But perhaps my greatest pleasure was in meeting the great American comedian, Jack Benny. During the short run of *After the Rain* in New York I had been asked by a rather pious lady in a television interview to name my favourite actor. I had replied 'Jack Benny', and since the pious lady had protested – probably expecting me to choose a distinguished theatrical knight – I had then enlarged on the subject. This interview had been reported to Mr Benny who made a special point of seeing *Hadrian* on his visit to London, and coming backstage after the performance. We sat together and talked about comic acting, in which he was one of the world's leading specialists.

My chief interest in the theatre is comedy and, since I regard *Hadrian VII* as primarily a comic performance, I will try to write about comic acting.

*

One of the most astonishing moments I have ever experienced in a theatre was during a performance by Jack Benny at the London Palladium. He was appearing with a team of associate performers, one of whom was the singer Phil Harris. Mr Harris had his own spot in the show and sang a group of songs, at the end of which he received a tumultuous reception. During the cheering and applause – which Mr Harris accepted rather like a triumphant boxer – Jack Benny quietly walked on to the back of the stage and stood and listened. He did nothing else. He just listened to the applause and jealously watched Mr Harris taking his bows. Gradually the audience noticed him and started to laugh, and the applause and cheering slowly changed into uncontrolled hilarity. The laughter went on and on as Benny stood watching Harris with beady eyes, and then looked askance at an audience who had bewilderingly enjoyed this simple-minded entertainment from one of his supporting cast.

The character of Jack Benny – or more accurately the well-known character that Jack Benny played – was that of an intelligent, normal, mean, vain and jealous man; for ever economizing and for ever being thwarted in his attempts. (Another of his great moments of comedy occurred in a sketch when a gunman held him up with the words, 'Your money or your life!' The pause which followed this demand was interminable, and the audience realizing Benny's predicament was helpless with laughter.) This character, which was combined with Benny's bland assumption that the rest of humanity was equally petty, and his astonishment that anyone should laugh at his frequent persecution and loss of dignity, made for irresistible comedy. It is a simple formula and he performed it with a simplicity that many actors envied and admired. He was able to amuse an audience as much with his thoughts as he did with his words, and his silences were often the most dazzling part of his performance.

Jack Benny

This thought-transference is for me one of the most interesting and challenging aspects of acting: the capacity to communicate with the minimum of expression; the ability to convey the thoughts and activities of a character by the simplest and cleanest of means. There must be absolute involvement and absolute clarity. Over-acting may amuse or even astound an audience for a little while, but it quickly becomes a bore. And a self-indulgent actor satisfies only himself.

The hardest acting is comic acting. There is of course an enormous amount of bad and mediocre comic acting which manages to please the uncritical. But good comic acting is the summit of an actor's art. To be believable in a ridiculous situation is twice as hard as to be believable in an uncomical situation. The ridiculous situation is nearer the borders of unreality – and if the actor once becomes unreal, the audience and the play are lost.

The comic character is also more complex than the so-called 'straight' character. There is nearly always some juxtaposition of elements in the personality and appearance that are at war with one another. For example, Benny's large sad eyes and innocent long-suffering face belied the meanness and the envy of his nature.

My favourite theatrical memories are nearly all of great comic acting.

The hypocrisy of John Gielgud dressed in immaculate mourning in *The Importance of Being Earnest* when he entered in a state of seemingly inconsolable grief for the death of an imaginary brother.

Rex Harrison in the New York production of *Venus Observed* battling wittily with his rampant sexuality and approaching old age.

Laurence Olivier in *Richard III* brilliantly contrasting his murderous activities with a slightly spinsterish deportment and manner of speech – superbly pointed by Shakespeare's marvellously descriptive verb 'to bustle'. 'God take King Edward to his mercy, And leave the world for me to bustle in!'

Ralph Richardson as Falstaff, using his immense size and nobility to counterpoint the character's cowardice and lewd preoccupations. (Paradoxically, this performance had a great tragic highlight. At the moment when Doll Tearsheet asks, 'When wilt thou leave fighting o' days and foining o' nights, and begin to patch up thine old body for heaven?' Richardson stood up, stepped forward and looked into eternity. 'Peace, good Doll! do not speak like a death's-head; do not bid me remember mine end.' The theatre was hushed and time stood still.)

Ruth Gordon as the widow in *The Matchmaker*, hiding her grief with a smiling clown's mouth painted nearly from ear to ear, as she deviously hooked a second husband while energetically matchmaking him with every other woman in sight. 'You go *your* way, and I'll go *mine*,' she said – pointing twice in exactly the same direction.

Irene Worth's monstrous American matron – Hitler in drag –

getting her come-uppance in Noël Coward's *Suite in Three Keys*.

Paul Scofield's gay hairdresser in *Staircase*, facing calamity and suppressing hysteria at the sight of his friend's new wig.

Syd Field – perhaps the greatest talent that I have ever seen – sitting at a table with the psychiatrist in *Harvey* and slowly becoming aware that the psychiatrist was holding his hand. This was a comic situation that seems in retrospect to have gone on for minutes, with Field slowly looking at the table and his imprisoned hand, and then slowly out front looking in vain for rescue; and then gradually and delicately releasing himself without the psychiatrist noticing his escape.

Syd Field was an exceptional Music Hall comedian because he could play more than one character with equal success: a simpleton being taught to play golf or billiards; a cockney spiv; or an effeminate photographer taking pictures of his best friend. But most comedians play only one basic role, and they play it to perfection. Jack Benny's tight-fisted dupe; Chaplin's tramp; W. C. Fields's drunken charlatan; Groucho Marx's lecherous anarchist. (The tragedy of Tony Hancock was that he became bored with the character that had made him a success and, ambitiously, he tried to become a more versatile entertainer – losing both his way and his public.)

I have learnt so much from watching the great acting comedians of the Music Halls and early cinema (I am not talking here of great clowns like Danny Kaye or Harry Secombe. This is a different art) and there is very little difference between their problems and the problems of the 'legitimate' actor working in 'straight' comedy. Their material is certainly broader, but the intensity of their involvement must be all the greater for this very reason. And their ability to hold a huge audience spellbound for long periods of time – sometimes completely on their own – is an awesome achievement.

There was for instance the bliss of watching the incomparable Max Miller, playing the part of the Cheeky Chappie, and confiding to a delighted and tremendously flattered audience the sexual exploits of himself and his numerous acquaintances. When Max Miller stepped on to the stage you knew that you could sit back and relax with absolute confidence. You knew without any doubt that you were going to be superbly entertained for at least forty minutes. He would appear wearing an outrageous satin or silk golfing suit ('Well, what if I *am*!') walk to centre stage and watch the mechanically worked microphone disappear ('Must be the cold weather!') then place one foot over the footlights and begin. He had absolute command over an audience – and this was not due to the brilliance of his material (hearing this on gramophone records much of it is relatively feeble) but to the brilliance of his delivery; in fact to his acting. Nobody could tell a secret like Max Miller. Nobody could change the subject like Max Miller. And nobody could boast so outrageously and disarmingly – 'the true gold of the Music Hall, lady!' – in the middle of his act to an audience who needed no convincing. As he frequently reminded us: 'There'll never be another!'

What was the secret?

Reality.

When Jack Benny stepped on to the stage at the London Palladium and made an audience helpless with laughter simply by standing still and watching a colleague receive applause, it was because we genuinely believed that he was jealous. We genuinely believed that this carefully built up situation was unrehearsed, and that it was an embarrassing revelation of petty malice which we all recognized with guilty delight as part of our own make-up.

When Jerry Desmonde yelled at Syd Field during the famous golfing sketch 'Make the tee!', received a blank stare and yelled again 'Make the tee with *sand*!' we genuinely believed Field's incomprehension and the logic of his reply: 'I'm not drinking *that stuff* – more like *cocoa*!' It looks like pitiful comedy material on paper, but the performance was genius.

If Max Miller had ever lost his relish for the tales he told, if Chaplin had not convinced us of his poverty, if the milk of human kindness had ever diluted W. C. Fields's monstrous cheating charlatan, if Frankie Howerd was not actually outraged by the behaviour of his fellow human beings, if Eric Morecambe was not so gloriously and believably gullible, their comedy would be diminished.

Their comedy would be diminished because we would no longer believe in them. It would be an unreal performance.

Despite the obvious lessons to be learnt from these great entertainers, many straight actors approach comedy as if it was some kind of holiday. Because *they* see the joke, they imagine that it will also amuse the audience. They think that it is sufficient for them to describe or illustrate a comic situation instead of *making it happen*. Good comic acting is very hard work, and the actor needs to wear blinkers to avoid seeing the humour. A splendid example was the complete involvement and superb humourless pomposity of Arthur Lowe's performance in the television serial *Dad's Army*.

The best performance of a farce which I have ever seen in England was directed by a Frenchman, Jacques Charon. This was the National Theatre production of *A Flea in her Ear*, which I saw early on in its run. In particular I can still vividly recall the amazing tragic frenzy of Geraldine McEwan and Frank Wylie, but there were at least half a dozen performances played with the energy and seriousness demanded of King Lear.

This is the heart of the matter.

Ralph Lynn said: 'The essence of farce is worry.'

Chaplin said: 'If what you're doing is funny, don't be funny doing it.'

This is the problem, and this is the fascinating challenge of comedy. This is why it is often the actors with the least sense of humour who are most successful. There is also the paradox of the lugubrious and sometimes even unpleasant off-stage personalities of many of the great Music Hall comics. Comedy must be related to tragedy. A good comedian must have experience of persecution and frustration. It is no coincidence that many of the best comics are Jewish – or that there is now a growing number of marvellous black comedians in America.

Why the English do not respect great comedy as much as they revere great tragedy is an interesting mystery. There seems to be some confusion that what is funny is lightweight and less worthy of consideration. This is not true of the great English novels, but – as Shaw complained – it is certainly true of the theatre, both of the work of playwrights and performers.

It was not long into the run of *Hadrian VII* before I began to have my own problems of sustaining a comedy performance. It was not long before I started to lose my original seriousness, and thus to lose some reality. After the silence of rehearsals and the nervousness of the early performances, the sound of laughter started its seduction. I began to find new laughs, and then I sensed that the play was beginning to lose some of its original impact particularly in the second act. It could only be my fault.

The sound of laughter is delicious, but it is an imperfect gauge of a good performance. On stage, one tends to count laughs, to measure the volume and the length of the reaction. Sitting in an audience, I have often laughed at a play or a performance until a certain moment when the play or the performance no longer seems funny. It just seems silly. Reality has been lost. Perhaps one will go on laughing, but with a growing resentment and resistance. And at the end of the evening, instead of feeling stimulated and refreshed, one is just plain tired. I sensed that this was beginning to happen to audiences with *Hadrian*.

There followed that desperate search for an explanation, and those dreadful post-mortems relished by all actors – and such a bore for everyone else. Is it slower? Am I gabbling? Is the theatre too hot? Has the standard of the audiences gone off already? ('They looked awfully old!') Is it really me? Perhaps it's someone else's fault! Am I antagonizing them? ('Nobody's been round for the last three performances!')

The answer is nearly always quite obvious, but it is the last thing that will occur to the actor. The answer in this case was the prime foundation of my performance – which I thought that I still had – until Peter Dews come to see the play and told me that I had lost it.

The early part of the play was fine. Here, there was a relatively simple situation of revenge, and the whip-lash wit of the character demanded a savagery of delivery which kept me on the right lines. But in the second half, after being elected Pope, the character mellowed and became much more complicated. This half of the play was funny because of the appearance of the dreadful little man of Act One now dressed as Pope and behaving as a sweet authoritative father figure – with only occasional lapses into schoolboy behaviour and his old vitriolic self. There was just one element of the character that went right through the play – and this was the element that I had lost. It was his Faith. Unless the character truly believes in God, despite his persecution, despite his arrogance, despite his cruelty and his wit, the whole basis of the role falls to pieces and just becomes a dazzling bit of camp nonsense.

Once a play starts a long run, the actor becomes more and

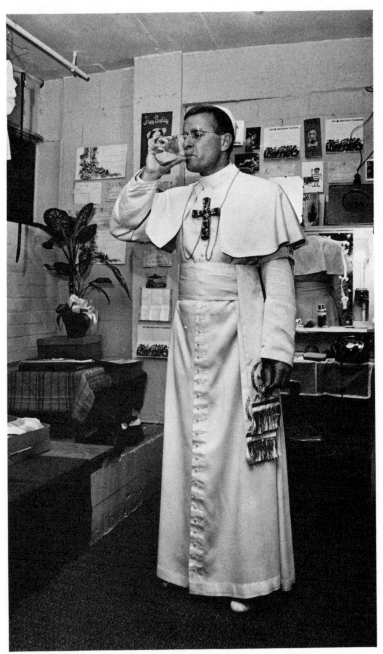

Prepared for the second half

more interested in details, and tends to forget the basic intentions of the role. I had based my performance on the assumption that Rolfe's fundamental intention was to serve God. His behaviour often seemed at odds with this, and it was all too easy to become immersed in the quirks and eccentricities of the man. But unless one believes that he is basically a devout man, his personality and his behaviour finally become tiresome and self-indulgent. Unless there is the juxtaposition of his deep faith in God on the one hand, and his irreverence towards the clergy and downright hatred of most of the rest of humanity on the other, the comedy of the play is diminished. This obvious but elusive element was disappearing from my performance, although of course it was not noticed by people seeing the play for the first time. They still seemed satisfied. However, after being made aware of the problem, and after attempting to repair the damage and put back the missing element of sincere faith – as opposed to the synthetic attitude that had crept in – the result was astonishing. Audiences started to cheer again, and, slowly, the fatigue I was beginning to feel completely disappeared. It is true that audiences laughed less in certain places – but they enjoyed themselves much more.

This is one of the terrible traps of comedy acting. It is very natural for the actor to equate the amount of laughter his character receives, with the success of his performance. It is not true. To act well in comedy you must not only make an audience laugh – you must make them laugh in the right places, and you must resist the temptation of making them laugh all the time. In fact to act well in comedy you must be very clever indeed.

David Garrick summed it up with his well-known advice to a young actor who begged to be allowed to play comedy: 'No, no! You may humbug the town sometime longer as a tragedian, but comedy is a serious thing.'

*

Far from having a minority appeal, the play attracted a much more varied audience than any of us expected. In particular, I found that audiences were stimulated by the play's examination of the challenge of practical Christianity and the failure of the Church to implement the teaching and instructions of Christ; the gap between the lip-service paid by the vast majority of Christians to the uncomfortable demands made by Jesus, and their actual behaviour in everyday life. It seemed very strange to me that people – sometimes even the clergy – could be surprised by this; as if it had never occurred to them before that Christ really meant what He said.

In particular, Hadrian's instruction to a Cardinal to 'starve and go to heaven!' and his intention at the end of the play of giving away the Vatican treasure, seemed to astonish and delight people. I could understand this surprising non-Christians and the ignorant, but the fact that it seemed to surprise a number of the apparently devout amazed me. It is not as if Christ's remarks and instructions on the subject are ambiguous.

'Lay not up for yourselves treasures upon earth . . .'

'Provide neither gold, nor silver, nor brass in your purses . . .'

'If thou wilt be perfect, go and sell that thou hast, and give to the poor, and thou shalt have treasure in heaven.'

'But woe unto you that are rich! for ye have received your consolation.'

But there seemed to be large numbers of people – and some of them wore dog-collars – who were startled by the idea that these sayings should be taken literally.

'And why call ye me, Lord, Lord, and do not the things which I say?'

Certainly none of the clergy – of any denomination – who came to the theatre were offended by the play, and perhaps the most memorable occasion during the run at the Mermaid was the special matinée we gave for the Lambeth Conference.

The idea of this performance came from Canon John Taylor, general secretary of the Church Missionary Society, and the audience included the Archbishop of Canterbury, Dr Ramsey; the Archbishop of York, Dr Coggan; the Apostolic Delegate, Archbishop Cardinale; and over 300 bishops and their wives. Bernard Miles decided to give them a warm-up before the play began and told a few of his best tales, and the actual performance was so well received that it really reminded me of the old radio programme, *Worker's Playtime*. Just as in that programme any remarks or insults addressed to the foreman or the management were received with delight, so Hadrian's corrosive attacks on the hierarchy were applauded and cheered. Many lines that received little or no reaction from lay audiences were seized on with delight, and there seemed to be general good-humoured agreement when I complained that: 'The clergy are *more*, not *less* human, and they are certainly not the pick of humanity.'

After the performance the publicity department begged me to dress up in my Pope's robes to meet the Archbishop of Canterbury. Owing to Bernard's warm-up at the beginning of the afternoon, the serving of tea and cakes during the interval, and the enormous amount of laughter during the show, the Archbishop was already late for his next appointment and decided that he couldn't wait. As I came out of the side entrance of the Mermaid, he was just walking down the alley towards his car. The publicity girl was frantic: 'Run! Run!' she demanded. 'No!' I replied, smugly aware of the newsreel and television cameras that were focused on me. 'The Pope cannot be seen running after the Archbishop of Canterbury!' Luckily somebody told Dr Ramsey that I was ready, we compromised on distance and greeted each other with dignity, surrounded by excited and bemused bishops.

It was an extraordinarily good-natured occasion, and of course the resulting publicity caused even longer lines at the box-office.

The Bishop of Cariboo, Dr Ralph Dean, said: 'The play has a great message for the Anglican Church, as it gets the priorities of the Church right – that of people before property.'

A happy discovery.

During the summer there was a good deal of talk about an American production of *Hadrian*, and because of the seasonal tradition of Broadway, this had to be carefully timed. Ideally, it is best to open a play in New York in the autumn, in the hope that it will run through the winter and spring. When the New York summer arrives only very successful plays can survive; the humidity and heat empty the city of tourists. The later a play opens in the season – that is to say in the winter or spring – the less are its chances of getting back the money spent on it. It takes much longer in New York before a play actually starts to *make* money because of the far greater costs. (It was nearly four months, playing to full houses, before *Hadrian VII* started to make money in New York.) If we were to catch the 1968–69 season, the sooner we could mount a production, the better the box-office prospects. However, I was reluctant to leave the

With the Rt Rev. Trevor Huddlestone (now Bishop of Stepney) at the Lambeth Conference matinée of *Hadrian VII*

London cast until I had played for at least six months – and I also knew that I would need a holiday before starting rehearsals all over again with a new company. It was decided that the latest possible date for opening would be Christmas, and arrangements were made accordingly. First of all Peter Dews had to find a replacement for me in London, rehearse him and see him settled in; then Peter had to cast the American company and have the play redesigned for a much bigger theatre. American Equity would not allow any other English actors except me to go with the play, and it meant starting again from scratch.

My last night at the Mermaid on 2 November was a very emotional affair, and when Peggy Aitchison in her role of the friendly charwoman bade me goodbye during the play, we both burst into tears on stage. After the performance there was a little party and the company gave me a portable tape-recorder for a present. They had all recorded messages on it.

It had been a wonderful run, though I was relieved that I would no longer have to do the play twice-nightly on Thursdays and Saturdays – with only a fifteen-minute break between performances. This was a marathon that left me almost dead with fatigue. I often stumbled out of the theatre too tired even to hail a taxi, and walked like a zombie along Fleet Street. But apart from this, it had been a very happy time with a very friendly company, and it was an enormous wrench to leave them.

I had four weeks off before starting rehearsals in New York.

After months of appearing in a play eight times a week the sudden freedom from responsibility is wonderful. It is not only the responsibility of giving a good performance every evening, or – as with *Hadrian* – the responsibility of leading a large company, it is the boring responsibility of looking after oneself and keeping oneself in immaculate running order. A performer – like a sportsman – relies on his own body to earn his living. Most people are able to function in their work even if they themselves are not 100 per cent fit. But an actor is himself the instrument of his work, and great care has to be taken of the complicated machinery.

The joy of sudden freedom is the relief from this nagging worry; the relief that it is not very serious if you catch cold, have a sore throat, have a sleepless night, use up all your energy during the day instead of saving it for the evening; it is not a disaster if you have indigestion or a hangover; and your behaviour does not have to approximate to a descriptive review displayed in large letters in the front of the theatre. In other words you can be a slob.

Also, during a long run, I feel a sense of claustrophobia. I long to get away from the judgement of audiences; away from my costumes and make-up, and above all away from my dressing-room mirror. I long for fresh air, space and anonymity.

On the Monday, after sending a good-luck telegram to my successor, Douglas Rain, I drove to Malvern, climbed to the top of the Hills and watched the sun set. The next day found me at a Chrysanthemum Show in Weston-super-Mare. Then I went over the moors to Plymouth to say goodbye to my family. If the play was successful in New York I was contracted to be away for ten months.

On my return to London, I made arrangements about letting my flat, sold my car, did Christmas shopping and said goodbye to friends.

It was during this time that I was pursued by a reporter and photographer from the American magazine *Look*. I was most uncooperative and refused to allow them to photograph me 'relaxing with friends'. They then followed me around and – fearing that I *had* no friends – tried to catch me talking with shop-assistants or taxi drivers. There was one occasion when I had gone into town to collect my ticket when they pleaded with me to feed the pigeons in Trafalgar Square, and look as if I belonged to one of the many families there. I actually spoke to a little girl, but she burst into tears and *Look* gave up.

For more space and fresh air I decided to travel by sea. On 23 November I sailed to Quebec on the *Empress of Canada*. It was one of the roughest crossings on record.

Luckily, since I had a few days to spare, my friend, Timothy Findley, the Canadian novelist and playwright, had asked me to stay at his farm in Cannington, Ontario, before starting rehearsals. It was a gorgeous weekend; sleeping in a huge brass-knobbed bedstead, walking the dogs in the snow, and gradually recovering from the terrible week tossing on the Atlantic.

Then I flew to New York.

New York

In 1969, being a successful actor in a hit play in New York still seemed more important than being a successful actor in a hit play in London. It was still necessary to conquer The Great White Way – even though that renowned thoroughfare was getting a little grey.

To the producers, a smash hit on Broadway is a passport to the sale of the movie rights. In America one belongs to the theatre industry – in England, only to the theatre business. In America an artistic success is admired, but a financial success is admired and respected. At that time theatre tickets cost nearly twice as much as in London; production costs were at least four times as much; and a star salary in a Broadway play is far bigger than it is in London – although over half of this disappears in tax. (Federal tax, State tax, City tax, Social Security and Trade Union dues are all deducted from one's pay packet.)

There was, therefore, a sense of embarking on an even greater adventure with the production of *Hadrian VII* in New York. The fever became contagious – and although I tried to fool myself that it didn't really matter, that London was my home and that nothing could compare with the perfect success I had had at the Mermaid – nevertheless I desperately wanted the play to succeed again for all our sakes. There was the memory of the long-rejected script, the faith and persistence of Peter Luke, the daring investment of Bill Freedman and Charles Kasher, the financial disaster at Birmingham, and the enormous amount of love and work that Peter Dews and I had put into it. We wanted an English success to become an international success. ('Think big!')

This was my seventh trip to New York. The first had been in 1948 when, as an enthusiastic but unsubtle young actor, I saw Elia Kazan's production of *A Streetcar Named Desire* and marvelled at the breath-taking performances of Marlon Brando, Jessica Tandy, Karl Malden and Kim Hunter. Since that eye-opening occasion I had been thrilled by so many great

American performances: John Garfield in *Skipper Next to God*, Julie Harris in *The Lark*, Edward G. Robinson and Martin Balsam in *Middle of the Night*, Fredric March and Florence Eldridge in *Long Day's Journey into Night*, Henry Fonda, Patricia Neal, Judy Garland, Ethel Merman . . . It would be good to succeed in their city.

New York!

I was feeling strangely cool, calm and confident when the plane landed at Kennedy Airport – perhaps even a little bloody-minded. This time I would *not* become embroiled in the usual Broadway hysteria. I would remain quietly detached, friendly, and amazingly kind. People would marvel at my contained and civilized demeanour. I think the performance lasted all the way to the hotel.

At the Meurice, Donald the doorman greeted me warmly: 'Mr McGowan! Welcome back!' The youngest and cheekiest of the elevator men took my bags and asked if I had got my 'Pope-kit' packed inside them. Dolores at the switchboard called out: 'How are you, darling?' – and I knew that I was home.

In the sitting-room of my suite, standing in front of the huge gaping fireplace stood a large tropical plant from the producers, Lester Osterman and Richard Horner. And on the polished table was a bottle of whisky from my new agent, Leo Bookman. There was also a pineapple.

I unpacked, and then went to have dinner at the Russian Tea Room with Peter Dews and his wife, and Bill Freedman. I was now feeling rather shaky, but was soon revived by a Bull-shot and an enormous steak. We talked excitedly of the new cast, the changes in staging, and backstage conditions in the new theatre.

Then I went back to the hotel and called up a few friends. Most of them congratulated me on my performance in advance – which made me very nervous. My agent rang to welcome me. The press-agent rang to make some appointments. The stage-manager rang to give me the rehearsal call. The lights of the crazy challenging city twinkled through the window. The noise of traffic drifted up. I switched the television on and off, and found I had a raging thirst. The pineapple caught my eye. There was as yet no cutlery in the kitchen drawer. I searched frantically for an implement to cut the gorgeous fruit. Finally, I carved it up with a tiny pair of nail scissors and made an awful mess. There was juice running down my face; I had a torn fingernail and stains all over my new jacket. Then, to combat the intense central heating, I battled hysterically with a window which had not been opened for years; and – without a trace of civilized or contained demeanour – went to bed.

The next morning I had breakfast at Horn & Hardart on 57th Street; bought coffee, sugar, fruit juice, milk, cookies and apples for my kitchen; and went to look at the squirrels in Central Park. My agent, Leo Bookman – of Heseltine, Bookman and Seff – took me to lunch at a restaurant called the Fontana di Trevi. He seemed to be a delightful man with a totally untheatrical personality. He said he had started out to be a professional baseball player, and had then studied dentistry for two years – until he decided that he didn't like looking into people's mouths. Then he drifted into the theatre scene. I was so fascinated that we were late for the first rehearsal.

This was at the Morosco Theatre. I walked in through the front of house and saw a crowd of nearly forty strangers staring down at me from the stage. Peter Dews introduced me to all of them and only forgot one name. I smiled like a lunatic. Chairs were placed all over the stage and I went to sit in the back row, but Peter called me out and made me sit on a throne in the front next to him. Then we read the play. As at Birmingham, I started to read in a flat monotone, not trusting my voice to obey me; but soon I caught one of the Swiss Guards yawning and, with pitiful vanity, I began to ham it up.

I was particularly glad to meet one of the actors, Gillie Fenwick, who was playing Dr Courtleigh, Cardinal-Archbishop of Pimlico. He had been a member of a weekly repertory company in my home town of Tunbridge Wells in 1939. As a stage-struck schoolboy of fourteen I had seen him act in many plays. Knowing that we were going to meet, I had brought over an old programme of the play *George and Margaret* in which he had appeared, and told him, quite truthfully, that he was the first good actor that I had ever seen. After the war he had moved to Canada, and Bill Freedman, who is also from Canada, had suggested him for *Hadrian*. The cast included three other Canadian actors, William Needles, Gerard Parkes and Peter Jobin, and several English actors who were now living in New York, so there was hardly any problem with accents.

According to my diary, the following day there was 'torrential rain and, unable to get a taxi or a bus, I ran to the theatre – not wanting to be late again. Arrived absolutely drenched. After an hour's work I selfishly said I was thirsty and everything stopped for coffee. Then the singers arrived to learn the "Christus Vincit" and we had to leave. Lunched at the Piccadilly Coffee Shop with Bill Needles and Roderick Cook – my understudy. I ate a huge salad and still felt very hungry. Must try to resist New York starch. Did very good work in the afternoon, and realized that during the London run I have become very vocal, and am often saying things purely for the effect of the words and not to convey the meaning. Peter Dews in riotous form, pouring forth direction and funny stories alternately.

'Had a bourbon on the rocks at the Theatre Bar to clinch the fact that I am actually here, and spent the evening with Gil Parker, talking shop and watching an enjoyably bad TV play. On the way home my elderly taxi driver shouted at a frail old woman who was slightly obstructing his way: "Drop Dead!" – not like Tunbridge Wells!'

Before leaving England I had cunningly asked Peter Dews if I could have a long weekend off during the American rehearsals; preferably at the end of the second week when the rest of the cast would still be learning their lines and I would not be missed too much. He had kindly agreed. So, at the end of the second week, I left the bitter cold of the city and flew to Florida for five days to stay with friends in Coral Gables.

On the plane, after two or three very strong cocktails, I was starting to nod off when a voice said: 'Can I have your autograph, please!' Greatly flattered at being recognized, I reached for my pen and turned to find that the autograph hunter was actually speaking to a well-known American Sports Writer who was sitting in the seat behind me. Caught with a pen in my hand – *I* asked for his autograph too.

It was a very refreshing weekend. I swam, sunbathed, went to several parties and, not being able to escape show-business entirely, saw the well-known dolphin 'Flipper' do his one-man show. There was a particularly memorable Sunday brunch given in my honour with Bull-shots and barbecued hamburgers round the swimming pool, a Christmas tree in the window, and a record of Vera Lynn singing 'There'll always be an England' blaring out of the loudspeakers.

Glowing with health after the weekend, I returned to find New York in the throes of the Hong Kong flu epidemic. Peter Dews was white-faced and sneezing, and already we had lost a couple of Cardinals. Morale was at a low ebb, and things were not helped by the fact that we were rehearsing in a ghastly crumbling cold hotel which smelt strongly of stale curry.

It was inevitably at this time that the American actors heard *their* outburst from Peter. One of them was having great difficulty learning his part and rehearsals were being held up by this. Suddenly came the breaking of the sound barrier. 'LEARN YOUR LINES!' – and another piece of hotel masonry crumbled.

It soon became obvious that the actress playing the part of the charlady was not up to it, and that she would have to be replaced. I spent a bizarre morning with Peter in Lester Osterman's Broadway office reading with various ladies who arrived wearing whatever they imagined were the right clothes and make-up for an English char. Some of them assured us they were Londoners – but they produced accents which we had never heard before. One after another they came, until I began to think that London must be 30,000 miles away, and Cockney a defunct accent from another age. Finally, however, a delightful

Outside the Helen Hayes Theatre

little dumpling of a lady called Marie Paxton walked in, and the search was over. She was the real thing.

There were to be thirteen previews at the Helen Hayes Theatre before the official first night; the first preview was cruelly set for Boxing Day, the 26th December. There was no cruel intention; Americans do not observe Boxing Day as a holiday – in fact most of them have never heard of it.

I spent most of Christmas Day with Peter and Anne Dews – or 'Mr and Mrs Doo' as the doorman called them – and in the evening, the English actress, Carole Shelley, invited us to a superb Christmas dinner, but I was so nervous I didn't wait for crackers.

In the notorious Venice letters of Fr Rolfe is the wonderfully innocent complaint: 'Neither beef nor turkey nor plum pudding nor mince pies have passed my lips, and I *adore* them all.' He could have had all of mine that night.

The previews proceeded successfully – with only small problems like bad acoustics in certain parts of the theatre, and the discovery that the vermilion of my new Papal slippers was so eye-catching against the white of my robes that Peter suggested changing the title to 'The Red Shoes'.

The build-up of nervous tension mounted as the first night approached and, to divert myself, I spent hours searching for suitable prints as presents for the company in the Museum of Modern Art, the Frick, and the Metropolitan.

Then they decided to take the pressure off the first night and invite critics to the play on the Monday and Tuesday – as well as on Wednesday, the official opening. At first I thought this a good idea, but the strain proved to be frightful – and that opening week in New York was one of the hardest I have ever spent in the theatre.

On Monday, Clive Barnes (*New York Times*) came to the play, and such is the power of the *Times* critic that this was perhaps the most important performance of all. Although he had already given us a rave review when he came to the Mermaid, there was no guarantee that he would do so again. Maybe I had grown glib in the role; maybe the new supporting cast would not please him; maybe he would make the favourite comment that 'the play has not survived the trip across the Atlantic'; or maybe we just wouldn't do it very well that night. I was so nervous in the first scene that one of my contact lenses popped out and dropped on to the floor; something that had never happened to me before. I decided to stop the action and stooped to pick up the tiny precious object. I don't know what this strange grovelling can have looked like from the front, but the necessity of doing something specific calmed my nerves and helped me to concentrate – although it was very puzzling for poor William Needles and Gillie Fenwick who were on stage with me at the time.

After the performance, a happy Peter Dews came backstage and pronounced it a good show; not the best he had ever seen, but certainly not the worst. Then he and I sat in my dressing-room, finished a bottle of whisky together, and staggered up 7th Avenue, stopping off for an enormous plate of waffles and molasses on our way back to the Meurice – where the night staff waited to hear our verdict. 'How'd it go, Mr Doo?' and, 'Did they like it, Mr McGowan?'

On Tuesday morning I was interviewed by *Time Magazine*, and had lunch at the Oak Room with Larry Dalzell who had flown over for the first night. Richard Watts, critic of the *New York Post*, came to the play that evening.

Wednesday, I had lunch with my American cousins from Cleveland who had flown to New York especially for the occasion, bringing with them their famous local columnist, Howard Wertheimer. I was very poor company; my eyes were glazed and my thoughts were elsewhere, and in answer to Mr Wertheimer's question: 'When did you begin acting?' I replied: '7.30 tonight.'

At the theatre we all went through the old ritual of terrifying each other with good wishes. My dressing-room was stacked with presents, cards and telegrams, and a reporter from the *New York Times* was posted backstage to watch a theatrical triumph or disaster.

It went very well.

Afterwards, in my dressing-room, Helen Jacobson, the producer of *After the Rain*, was the first to greet me. She then asked to go to my lavatory and, with the crush that followed, she was trapped inside for twenty minutes. Old friends and total strangers crowded into the tiny room. A photographer tried to take pictures, and the *New York Times* reporter tried to take down copy. When they had all left, he followed me to Sardi's for the first-night party. I entered to prolonged applause, shoulder-slapping and handshakes and found it all enjoyably embarrassing. I also found that with the unexpected overflow of guests there was nowhere for me to sit. Finally, Larry Dalzell gave me his chair, his supper and his drink, and one of the American actors told me: 'We got two favourables.' The producers asked me to go up to the offices and watch the other TV reviews, but I preferred to stay with the company and my American cousins.

When the *New York Times* appeared there was more applause and rejoicing, and a brand new line of people formed to congratulate me. This time there was a large number of lawyers and accountants among them.

Barnes wrote: 'Mr McCowen as Hadrian was the sensation of the London theater last season. This season he should be the sensation of Broadway,' and concluded his review, 'If you miss Mr McCowen in *Hadrian VII* I solemnly assure you, you will be missing one of the most fantastically alive performances of our decade.'

I couldn't ask for anything more – but it was impossible to stay up too late celebrating since there was a special matinée on Thursday, and many American actors would be coming to judge for themselves. This was yet another testing performance, luckily crowned by a visit backstage afterwards by one of my favourite American actresses, Julie Harris. In the evening there were out-of-town and magazine critics in the audience.

On Friday, I had an interview with Mel Gussow, a very intelligent writer for *Newsweek*; and, after the performance in the evening, another interview. This was with the most feared writer on the current show-business scene, Rex Reed, writing for the *New York Sunday Times*. The local members of the cast seemed terrified for me; the management were obviously very nervous, and a line of people came to bid me goodnight in the dressing-room with warnings such as 'Don't drink!' 'Don't swear!' and 'Don't let him see you're scared!' In actual fact I found Rex Reed delightful and amusing company, a self-confessed fan of theatre and films, and an extremely deft manipulator of an actor's ego. He left the hotel at 2 a.m. and I collapsed into bed. His article, when it appeared a week later, was very friendly – even though he made a good deal of fun of my behaviour and personality.

There were two shows on Saturday and, to complete the week,

Hirschfeld's caricature for the *New York Times*

on Sunday there were two parties given in my honour. I knew hardly anyone at either party except the hostesses – and realized that I had been 'caught' for exhibition. After standing for hours answering inane questions about the differences between New York and London, drinking too much and eating too little, being asked to relate the plot and explaining that Hadrian was not a real Pope nor a Roman Emperor, I made my escape and went back to the 5th Avenue home of my friend Gretchen Corbett who had been with us in *After the Rain*. She lit a log fire and made me beef consommé. I sat in an armchair with a shawl round my shoulders like a feeble old man and vowed that henceforth I would lead a quiet secluded life.

*

I am not normally a gregarious person, but living in New York during the months of *Hadrian* was an exceptional time. This is a typical month although mainly a catalogue of meals . . .

Monday, 3 February

Am a guest of honour at a Drama Desk Luncheon (given by the critics) with Jerry Orbach and Donald Pleasence. Make a speech. Read the English Sunday papers. To Haymarket bar after the show with Gillie, Truman, Ted, B.J., and Joe Neal. Sandwich with B.J. on 8th.

Tuesday, 4th

Very boring lunch with a persistent old fan at Oak Room. Sit at the next table to David Merrick who complimented me on having 'come a long way' since *The Matchmaker* (which he produced). I retorted: 'I see you're still doing it' – referring to his musical version *Hello Dolly* – and he laughed. Meet Bill Needles at 2.30 and see a dreadful Italian movie. Buy some ties in Bloomingdales. Walk back to Meurice. After show to Gil's to meet and talk about acting to six drama students – and eat fondue.

Wednesday, 5th

Lunch with Gerald Holmes at hotel. Two shows. Meet Lindsay Anderson on my way home and have a cup of chocolate with him.

Thursday, 6th

Take Helen J. to lunch. Buy a book about the Lunts. After show turn down invitations to dine with Joan Fontaine or go to the 1st night party of *Dear World*, but went to W 72nd for supper with Clive and Patricia Barnes and John Wood.

Friday, 7th

Lunch with Sam Gordon at Mont St Michel. Run across the Park. To Guggenheim Museum and meet Bill Ritman. Supper with Norman Maibaum and Shirley at Lord Jim's.

Saturday, 8th

Lunch with Christopher Hewett. Matinée, and am bad tempered because of distractions in the wings. Dine on duck with Gillie and Gerard P. Meet some cousins from Miami. Nice. With Needles to 5th Avenue and supper with Gretchen, Paul Sparer and Nancy Marchand. Curry.

Sunday, 9th

Deep, deep snow. Traffic stopped and very quiet. To see the 1st half of *Lion in Winter* – pretentious muck. In eve to W 13th on subway to John Colenback and D.J. Watch a superb Fred Astaire spectacular.

Monday, 10th

Feel a bit poorly. Write letters. Bob Shattuck called in and took me walking in a transformed Central Park. Vivid blue skies and sheer white snow. Kids sleighing on trays and teenagers smoking pot. A poodle went crazy. To Howard Johnson's for a poached egg. Home and rest and read. Take Jim Shepherd to dine at Biaritz. Excellent. Nice show and drink with Bill and Gillie at Haymarket.

Tuesday, 11th

Do some shopping. Jack Benny phoned in the afternoon, and Joel Martin called round. After the show, Edgar Brown Jnr and a Miss de Winter took me to Forlini's in Baxter St, Chinatown. Friendly and empty. Hot seafood antipasta and talk about Jesus. A nice change!

Wednesday, *12th*

Go to the Sherry Netherlands at twelve to see Jack Benny. He gave me a gold money clip – inscribed, but without a dollar in it. He said he figured I didn't need one. He was very affectionate and happy. When I left I said, 'Take care!' – and really meant it. Went to Moores between the shows with Gretchen and had Irish Stew. Finally staggered home and made hot milk and took a sleeping pill.

Thursday, *13th*

Listen to a letter tape from England. Walk to E. 51st and lunched with Dewey and Lester at the Baroque Restaurant. Good food and decor unchanged since 1934. Back to hotel. Am visited by G.L. a very talkative writer. Am soon exhausted. Have eggs at the Ed Sullivan Coffee Shop. Celeste Holm came round with a nephew, and bitched elegantly. Had supper with John Schlesinger at Downeys, and swopped Ruth Gordon stories.

Friday, *14th*

Made phone calls. Victor Davis of the *Daily Express* came for an interview from 11 to 12.15. Then I walked to the Rockefeller Center Post Office and posted my tape; caught a taxi to Gramercy Square, had a sandwich with some students who were enthusing over an old Bette Davis movie seen on TV. Saw Steve McQueen in *Bullit*. He is marvellous. Walked up Lexington. Had a hot chocolate and a piece of lemon pie at a Choc-Full-O-Nuts. Met Bill Needles for roast beef at McGinnis's. Got hugged at the theatre for St Valentine's Day. Bit my tongue during the show, and my throat hurt from the cold weather. Bernard and Cora Gerstein came round afterwards for a drink. Then I caught the 8th Avenue bus to Central Park South and joined Truman Gaige, Gillie, Billy, Peter Jobin, Bill Bush and Leonard Soloway for gin, cheese, and an extraordinary Sophie Tucker record.

Saturday, *15th*

Quiet slow morning, and brunch at the hotel. Bus to theatre. Matinée. Buy *The Times*, and rest with a heat pad on my back which is giving stabs of pain. Hume Cronyn, and Michael York and his wife came backstage. Then I took a taxi to Christopher Street and a party of Maya Miles. Strange group. Neat gin and prawn curry. Go on to a Village bar and home on the subway at three.

Sunday, 16th

A little shakily into the Park for a short walk, then to Helen J.'s for brunch – with Jaimie and David. Have Danish Marys. Feel better. Dash down to see a bit of *Star*, and liked Dan Massey. Across the street to Bruce Monette for Southern Fried Chicken and a collection of people. There was a pet cobra, and conversation was mainly about old movies. Slept well.

Monday, 17th

To Radie Harris for coffee and to give her memories of Vivien Leigh. Lunch at Champignon with Joel. Rest in afternoon. Meet Lester and Marjorie Osterman at Moores for some rather indifferent haddock! Show – very energetic and much too funny. Then up to 93rd Street to L. and S. for supper. They had a nursery with two cats and a black rabbit . . .

Tuesday, 18th

A professor from Long Island University called round and talked for an hour – about himself. Then Veronica Laurie came for sherry and lunch at the Topkapi. In the afternoon I wrote many letters and read two plays and felt quite giddy. After the show to Bob Shattuck's apartment for supper with Marthe Schlamme. Gin and Nina Simone and home.

Wednesday, 19th

Eat at the hotel with all the matinée ladies. When I left I heard Donald the doorman telling some of them: 'That's Mr McGowan, the toast of Broadway!' Two shows – the second rather good. Home at 11.30 and hot milk and a pill.

Thursday, 20th

A lady from *Women's Wear* and a photographer came to 14 D for an interview and pictures. Lunched at the Barbizon Plaza with Dewey, Lester, and a nervous man from Tiffanys. Bull-shot, pork chops and Irish coffee. Feel great. To the agents to give back scripts. Letters. Have a hamburger at the Coffee Mill ('If I don't get some service soon I'm leaving!'). Strain a muscle in my back during the show. Eat with Bill Freedman at Chambers.

83

Friday, 21st

D.W. rang and I joined him to take the dogs, Leo and Samantha, for a walk. Then we lunched at Zum Zum's and had a banana split in Blums. Extraordinary cake-and-cream-hooked ladies; one of them reading a book called *Freaking Out*. D. said, 'A good trip on L.S.D. could be the equivalent of a year's analysis . . .' To Tiffanys to pick up a gold toothpaste key. Meet Peter Jobin, have a 7 Up, and see a Marlon Brando movie. Dinner at the Blue Ribbon. Start to tremble. Feel very depressed and give a very good performance. After the show Kerry Gardner took me to supper with Joseph Hardy. Soufflé, salad and champagne. Did not sleep.

Saturday, 22nd

After second show down to the Village for a party. Pot. Like the feeling of distance but not the flavour of the grass.

Sunday, 23rd

Wake at 10.30, giggling! Go for a gentle walk in the slush. Shattuck collected me and took me to the Village on the 6th Avenue subway. Had coffee and a begel. To see *Jacques Brel is alive and well and living in Paris*. Very enjoyable and sometimes moving. Back to 82nd St for a lovely evening. Gin and beef strogonoff and records. 'Little Green Apples' . . . and two big tears rolled down my cheeks. Am very homesick.

Monday, 24th

Take Brian Phelan to lunch at P J Clarke's. Rest and read papers. A very good easy show, and masses of people backstage. Am presented with the *Evening Standard* Award by Mr and Mrs John Coote in the dressing-room. Then sup with them at Sardi's.

Tuesday, 25th

Brian came over for coffee. Walk with him down 6th Avenue. To Act One for an interview with Joan Rubin for *Playbill*. Reminiscences of New York. Home, and read a film script of *The Blood Knot*. Show, decline invitations, and go to the Haymarket with the company. Feel good and active again.

Wednesday, 26th

Had a nice meal with Bill Needles and John between the shows.

After the second a party seemed to assemble in my room. Home late, exhausted.

Thursday, 27th

Lunched with Clint Singleton at the Fonda de la Sol in the Time-Life Building. To a matinée of *Does a Tiger wear A Necktie?* at the Belasco, with Pete, Bob and John Kramer. Very impressive acting from Roger Robinson, Al Pacino and Lauren Jones. Visit backstage. Hurry back to Meurice for a rest and a phone call. After show to Joe Allen's with Brian for steak and kidney pie (American style).

Friday, 28th

A bad night. Write letters in morning. Then with Bill Ritman to Museum of Modern Art. Take a punishing walk in the Park. Back to hotel and mope. Then give a highly comic performance! Ruth Gordon and Garson Kanin round ('What did ya do! Ya broke the atom!') and supper with them at Moores.

Saturday, 1st March

Walk to Downey's for lunch with John Roberts. Matinée. Jack Benny round for a hug. Have a rest. Roast beef in Moores. Jolly good show. Bob Kunst and Peter Steinberg round. Search for a cab. Subway to Village. Miss a folk-dancing display – thank God! To a fancy-dress party. Host and hostess dressed in luminous paint as 'blue meanies'. The dregs of some punch. No food. 'Enjoy yourselves!' A guest dressed as Christ in a crown of thorns with a trickle of blood running down his face sitting on a sofa necking. Host: 'Upstairs is the *real* fun.' Nothing but a log fire! Hostess: 'We're hoping to make a baby!' Leave. Am utterly alone – without food or drink. Have a stinger at the Studio bar. Play 'Little Green Apples' on the juke-box. Stupid old fool! Go to bed.

*

In retrospect this looks very hectic and – despite the social life – rather lonely.

It was sometimes lonely. There was a particularly bleak night after we had done our Actor's Benefit. All successful Broadway shows are expected to do a benefit performance for American Equity and, despite giving up a weekend, it is usually a very

pleasurable experience since the audience is mainly composed
of theatre people, and their reception of the play is very warm
and friendly. After our benefit performance, which was on a
Sunday afternoon, many American actors came backstage with
congratulations, but when they had all left I suddenly realized
that I was completely alone. The company had all gone home
and, stupidly, I had made no arrangements for the evening. The
theatre was empty except for the stage-door man. I stayed and
talked with him for a while and he did his cigar trick for me. Like
most New York stage-door keepers he had once been in
Vaudeville – and he loved to launch into his act or show the
faded photographs in his scrapbook. But this was obviously not
going to fill my evening. I walked outside and looked at the
front-of-house display, and then had that frightening feeling
that many actors have experienced of wondering if I was just a
name on a poster. I looked at the photographs of the person
cavorting around in Papal robes, sometimes stern, sometimes
laughing, sometimes screaming – and he seemed much more
real than me. He seemed to have more life than me, more
purpose and more colour. He was obviously – from the quotes
of the newspaper reviews – quite clever, and he was obviously
important enough to fill a large building for nights on end. But
then – who was I?

With no script and no plot and no character, I walked slowly
home and watched television.

But this was an exceptional occasion. I had been in love with
New York since my first trip in 1948, and have always felt vividly
alive in the concrete jungle; the smell of cigars and hot dogs and
perfume; the music of the record stores; the crowds of strangers
of every nationality; the canopies outside the bars and hotels;
the yellow taxi-cabs – invariably off-duty; and the marvellous
variety of villages and communities within the city. It is true that
I had not been to Harlem since 1952 and that there were now
several other areas that it was best to avoid. Many of the once-
loved hotels and restaurants were run down or pulled down.
Night life had diminished since the days when I saw Eartha Kitt
or Harry Belafonte for the price of a beer and a sandwich. The
Ziegfeld was gone. The Astor was gone. The Bon Soir was closed.
Central Park was unsafe at night. Madison Square Garden was
rebuilt. The Empire State Building was in eclipse. But there was
still the skating rink at the Rockefeller Center. The Plaza

Regards to Broadway in Times Square

retained its charm. 1st, 2nd, and 3rd Avenues had actually improved with the years. The sea lions still yelped at the zoo. In the summer of 1969 you could drink claret and eat steak tartare by the lake in Central Park. The little movie houses still showed those old double features with Katharine Hepburn and Cary Grant, Mae West and Cary Grant, Irene Dunne and Cary Grant. Off-Broadway thrived with forty little theatres playing anything from *The Boys in the Band* to Brecht. There was Joe Allen's and Charley O's and The Ginger Man. You could still see a liner leaving for Europe at the bottom of the street. Mabel Mercer and Bobby Short still sang.

At a Tony Award nomination party with Lauren Bacall, Sir John Gielgud and Zero Mostel

During the run of the play there was an assortment of events to fill my days: I went to many of those long lunches beloved of Americans, where awards and prizes for every possible achievement are handed out; I made an end-of-term speech to the students of The Neighbourhood Playhouse, and addressed various bodies ranging from 'The League of Directors and Choreographers' to 'The Lady Treasurers of the Box-Office'; I gave a poetry recital at the Poetry Center, and appeared as the mystery guest in *What's My Line* – where the panel guessed that I was James Earl Jones. On Thursday afternoons there was the *Hadrian VII* soft-ball team to cheer in Central Park. I was photographed in every possible position for *Harper's Bazaar* with two of their most ravishing models. And through the kindness of the splendid Irish actor, Neil Fitzgerald, I had a pixilated lunch with the poet, Padraic Colum, and attended a 'Pipe Night' at the Player's Club to honour James Cagney – who perversely elected to sing 'I'm an Old Cow Hand' in Yiddish.

Then, after the months of snow and slush, the excitement of the first warm day. There were weekends by the sea or in the country. Towards the end of May I had an invitation to spend a weekend on Fire Island, but since it was early on in the summer season there was no way of getting there after the show. Then I discovered that the producers of *Hair* were giving their entire company a weekend outing on the Island, and that they were leaving by coach after the show on Saturday night. I begged a lift. Leaving the ecclesiastical atmosphere of the Helen Hayes Theatre, I took my suitcase round to the stage door of the Biltmore and climbed in with the wild and friendly company. It was a good trip.

There were weekends with friends in West Chester, Pennsylvania, in Washington, and Long Island; and I will never forget the weekend spent with one of our producers Lester Osterman and his family at Darien, or the moment after lunch when I went to sleep by the watermill and Lester gently slipped a blanket over me.

There were always requests for interviews, especially from students and school magazines. There was the precocious fourteen-year-old schoolboy who made me blush when he insisted, 'There must be *some* moments when you feel very satisfied with yourself!' – and when I denied it, observed, 'Well you *seem* very self-satisfied!'

There were the cranks who asked for advice but really wanted an opportunity to talk about themselves. There was the aspiring amateur actor who did the whole of the handbag scene from *The Importance of Being Earnest* – playing both John Worthing and Lady Bracknell – in my hotel, and then demanded an unequivocal 'Yes' or 'No' as to whether he should give up his present job and join 'the theatre'.

There was the white-faced student who burst into my dressing-room after a performance and cried: 'Tell me, wasn't the first act a little down?'

There were the nuns who wanted to be photographed with Hadrian in his Papal robes, and the mysterious Monsignore who was most anxious for me to be his guest at a nearby Athletic Club.

Then there were many play and film scripts to read, and I had several strange offers of work to follow *Hadrian* ranging from a Japanese role in a musical, to directing a new play with Greer Garson.

But, chiefly, there was the company. Being the leading man of a large company offers a responsibility which is quite easily ignored, but which it is a good thing to accept.

It may not make much difference to the actual performance of a play if the actors are the members of a happy or an unhappy company. But there is an enormous difference in the everyday lives of all concerned, and there is an enormous difference between looking forward to one's work and dreading it.

I think the well-being of a company stems from the top, and that a leading actor can be a bridge between the rest of the cast and the management. This is particularly necessary in America where the unemployment is so terrifying that actors will often suffer indignities to retain their jobs. They are reluctant to complain about grievances and injustices that arise, for fear of jeopardizing their weekly pay packet or getting a bad name as a trouble-maker. If the leading actor is a readily available and sympathetic person, he can often arbitrate in these matters without any fears. I believe there is a tradition that a star dressing-room door should always be open, and that the rest of the company should always feel welcome.

But, quite apart from grievances (and there were very few with the *Hadrian* company), I am able to function much better in a friendly atmosphere, and I think it is a help to the performance of a play if even the humblest member of the cast has a sense of importance. I was delighted when the company visited me before or after the play simply for the pleasure of saying 'Hello' and relating the latest news. And I made a point of arriving early at the theatre every evening in order to have a cup of tea with Bill Needles and Gillie, and then pay my calls to various dressing-rooms. The longer the play ran, the greater was the feeling of a close-knit family with a keen desire to sustain a high standard of performance.

We were very lucky with *Hadrian VII* that the production staff were all very nice people. I value my permanent friendships with Company Manager, Leonard Soloway, Production Stage-Manager, Ben Janney, and Press Representative, David Powers. I was also blessed with another marvellous dresser, Ted August. He was ruthlessly efficient, fiercely protective and wickedly funny.

I played over 500 performances of *Hadrian* and, although I never grew tired of the role, I certainly grew tired. The necessity of giving eight performances a week gives rise to problems that have little to do with acting. How can one avoid anticipating the situations and dialogue of the play? How can one avoid a gradual decline into a rigidity of voice and gesture? *How can one be surprised?* The brain cannot wipe away the memory of a performance given only a few hours previously. An insult is as meaningless as a compliment if it is given with relentless repetition. Words disintegrate into gibberish, sense into nonsense, and the journey of a character in a play can become the journey of an idiot on a roundabout, propelled by mechanical necessity.

I used many ways to keep myself fresh, and tried to vary my approach to each performance. Sometimes I would concentrate on the relationships of the character; sometimes on each individual activity, and sometimes on the overall intentions. I also discovered a simple trick which seemed to be a great help. This was to literally imagine the fourth wall and to enclose myself in a geographical privacy. This counteracted the inevitable temptation to play out front and stray into false theatricality. The audience becomes a magnet and the actor is tempted to draw nearer and nearer towards them. But the reverse should be true. The actor should be the magnet and draw the audience to him.

I could happily have played *Hadrian* for the rest of my life if it could have been done amongst a repertory of other plays. But no matter how rich and complex a role may be, it is not possible to sustain a perfect standard of performance indefinitely with eight repetitions a week. The brain cannot be surprised with such frequency, and the necessary life-like reflexes have to be artificially stimulated. Some people will say that this is the job of a professional actor. It is indeed his job – but it must also be admitted that there is a vast difference in quality between a performance alive with nerves and adventure, and a performance which is battling with complacency and over-familiarity.

When my last night finally came, I hadn't the energy to be sorry. There was just a sense of relief. As the young priest says of the assassinated Hadrian: 'He was so tired . . .'

Five Years Later

ST MARK'S GOSPEL

'At least you're secure in your career, Mr McCowen.'

'Secure?' I shouted. 'Secure? – I'm trapped by my career! I'm imprisoned by it!'

It was the first time that I had protested with any emotion. It was the first time that I had shown any emotion.

This dialogue took place with my analyst Dr Thompson, at his home in Well Walk, Hampstead, in November 1974. I believed it to be 'the break-through'. It was 'the break-through' I had been trying to make for many months.

These things spring to my mind. This feeling of imprisonment in my career was a discovery that I needed to make. Intellectually I knew it. I had known it intellectually for a long time. But my loathing of the fact, the depth of my loathing of the fact, was the discovery.

I had never shouted at Dr Thompson before. I had never contradicted him so firmly. I had never revealed that I knew better than him in certain areas. And I had certainly never wept in front of him.

He looked most concerned and offered to make me a cup of tea. I accepted the offer.

I suppose that Dr Thompson was a good analyst for me because he represented the 'adult world' with the utmost rigidity. He seemed to be much more contained than me; much more knowledgeable; much more 'grown-up'; much more in charge of his life; and he presented a parallel with my childhood conflict; my early predicament that it was impossible to compete with the adult world of my father. I believed that I didn't belong in that world, and escaped to the make-believe world of the theatre. And now even that make-believe world had become a prison.

When he returned with my cup of tea (which I drank feeling like the victim of some fire or road accident) I asked him to get me out of my next job. I pleaded to be sent to a rest home in the country. I saw myself – immediately dramatizing the situation –

sitting beside a large log fire, with a shawl around my shoulders, drinking endless cups of sweet tea . . .

Dr Thompson agreed that he could get me out of my next job, but cannily suggested that we defer the decision until our next session together.

I staggered to the Hampstead Underground Station – I'd been afraid to drive the car – feeling most important and very delicate.

A stroll with Diana Rigg during rehearsals of *Pygmalion*

I had just completed a very successful six months' run as Professor Higgins in a West End revival of *Pygmalion* directed by John Dexter and playing opposite Diana Rigg.

The next job was as Alceste in an American season of the National Theatre production of *The Misanthrope* – also directed by John Dexter and playing opposite Diana Rigg.

That day it seemed to me unthinkable that I would ever do it.

*

Following the tremendous success of *Hadrian VII* in 1968 and 1969, I had played Hamlet with the Birmingham Rep.; the

The poster for *Butley*

With Peter Firth in *Equus*

leading role in Christopher Hampton's wonderful play *The Philanthropist* in London and New York; a season as Simon Gray's gloriously anarchic *Butley* at the Criterion Theatre; I created the part of Dr Martin Dysart in Peter Shaffer's sensationally successful play *Equus*; and played Alceste in Tony Harrison's acclaimed version of *The Misanthrope* at the National Theatre. I had also directed my first play, Terence Rattigan's

Pygmalion, with Ellen Pollock

While the Sun Shines at the Hampstead Theatre Club; and made two movies, *Frenzy* directed by Alfred Hitchcock, and *Travels with My Aunt* directed by George Cukor.

All these jobs had been successful. I was beginning to take success for granted. Not to succeed became unthinkable. I was a success machine.

But the machinery was wearing out. The strain began to mount during the rehearsals of *Pygmalion*. I was seized with panic, and the necessity to succeed became desperate. I didn't reveal this desperation to the cast or the director, but at home I was crippled with terror. One morning I collapsed with hysteria. Nevertheless, on opening night my performance was praised by audience and critics.

But already I began to dread the thought of going through the same process again. In the opening scene of *Pygmalion*, standing on stage waiting for my first cue, hidden behind a church pillar, my body would be leaden with inertia. I had no energy and no joy.

On the advice of Ellen Pollock – who played my mother, Mrs Higgins, in the play, and who became an invaluable friend – I tried to find comfort with Christian Science. But I did not persevere.

I went to a skilled masseur. It didn't help.

Finally, I saw my doctor and talked to him about my feelings, and he strongly recommended that I see an analyst.

I had met Dr Thompson fifteen years previously, and had assumed that he must be retired or dead, but he was vigorously alive, and the sessions started. They lasted throughout the run of *Pygmalion*, but it wasn't until the proposed season in America of *The Misanthrope* was only a few weeks away, that I actually expressed my determination to get out of my contract to do the job. I would not be able to find the passion to play Alceste. I had no passion left in me.

*

Of course, I went to America.

But I went reluctantly and grudgingly, not caring whether I failed or succeeded. And this was the first time that I had ever felt that way.

I was forty-nine.

Is there a link with the despondency that I felt at thirty-nine? At that time I certainly cared about failure or success, I just didn't know *how* I could or would succeed. And that despondency led to a premature embracing of professional middle-age and eventually to the success of *Hadrian VII*.

Now, faced with the irrevocable approach of half a century, my despair led me in many new directions, both personal and professional, and eventually to the strangest adventure of my life, a Solo Performance of St Mark's Gospel.

I agreed to go to America with *The Misanthrope*, doubtless helped by the guidance of Dr Thompson, and flew to Miami for a short holiday a few days before the rehearsals started.

I stayed with the friends I had visited during the rehearsals of *Hadrian VII*, and after a couple of days one of them bravely lent me a car, and I set out for Key West. Friends in England had recommended the drive from Miami to Key West, and my curiosity and ambition not to miss anything made me determined to make the journey.

It is not a long journey – about 120 miles – but it is one of the strangest journeys in the world. For a great deal of the way one is driving on a narrow road through the sea, going from one island reef – or Key – to the next, on a road bridge which was developed from the old Florida East Coast Railway. At one point there is a distance of seven miles from Key to Key.

Despite the novelty of the huge American car, despite driving on the right-hand side of the road, despite the terror of hitting enormous trucks coming in the opposite direction, I was thrilled by the journey. In some way, which I do not fully understand, it became a symbolic journey. And I kept many postcards of Key West and the Seven Mile Bridge. The postcards showed the road going on and on through the sea, and in the far, far distance, land ahead.

What does it mean?

Vertebrae?

Life-lines?

Or does the fact of my driving to Key West simply make an unexpected contrast with the gibbering invalid of a few weeks ago, staggering to the Hampstead Underground Station, hoping that the nice doctor would put him quietly away in a home for broken-down puppets? I don't know. But I felt the exhilaration of possible achievements again, and sniffed at new adventures.

In Key West I stayed at the Sun 'n' Surf Motel.

There was a sign by the sea which said: '90 Miles to Cuba'.

Soon after arriving I went for a swim, and noticed an attractive young couple. He was called to the phone, and when he returned he whispered in her ear. She cried out in terrible distress. He put his arm around her. They left the beach, packed and drove away. Somebody must have died. It was an inaudible drama.

That evening I explored the town.

It has one main street. On one side is Delmonico's (known as Tennessee Williams's bar), and on the other side is Sloppy Joe's

Seven Mile Bridge, in the Florida Keys.
My postcard of the Seven Mile Bridge

(known as Ernest Hemingway's bar). There were a few people in both bars, and they seemed to be in character.

The next day I did touristy things, and visited the Hemingway home – still filled with cats – and went for a guided tour.

At first the guide seemed to be a conventional old man, but he suddenly involved us in a strange scene. He drove us into a huge cemetery, stopped by a grave, and emotionally informed us that it was the final resting place of his lover. His lover had died exactly ten years ago, and he asked us to observe a minute's silence for him. We obeyed, and then continued with our tour.

There was another strange scene in Delmonico's that night.

Three men sat round the square-shaped bar in the middle of the room. The silence was appalling. A young barman called Luke tried his best to relax us, but no one was willing to contribute small talk. We drank and smoked. Suddenly, the door opened and a slim young girl of about twenty came and joined us at the bar. She wore a sexy off-the-shoulder white evening dress and carried a white gardenia. She asked for a glass of white wine, and also for a glass of water. She put the gardenia in the glass of water beside her, and carefully sipped the white wine. The silence continued for several minutes. Then a telephone rang. The telephone was on the bar and Luke answered it. He smiled and then said, 'Oh, it's you!' Then he looked at us and winked and started a cabaret conversation. Gradually we gathered that the caller was a schoolgirl who telephoned Luke regularly in the evenings when she was bored with her homework. She liked to flirt with Luke, but he was obviously not romantically interested in her. He asked her questions about her home life. He asked her if she had a brother. He asked her if she slept with him. She didn't. He asked her if she had a sister. He asked her if she slept with her. She did. Finally Luke told her to go back to her homework and leave him to his bar-tending. The schoolgirl asked if she could meet Luke later that night. He refused her. Then, suddenly, the slim girl in the white evening dress barked hungrily: 'Oh tell her to come on over! *I'll* show her a good time!'

It seemed as if all the locals were auditioning for Tennessee Williams.

On the plane to New York, the terror started again and I was convinced that I would never play Alceste in America. I would never get through rehearsals.

After about a week, the director, John Dexter, took me aside and said, 'The American actors and stage-management are getting awfully puzzled. Couldn't you at least raise your voice a little and let them know they've got a leading man.'

This appealed to my vanity. I started to raise my voice. Higher and higher. I started to relax. Passion – or something that at any rate passed for passion – returned. The American actors and stage-management were impressed. Each day my lungs took in more air, and the sheer muscular pain caused by those violent tirades gradually diminished. I got into trim again.

The strength needed to play many leading classical roles is enormous. Without gradually working towards the performance, one develops cramps and breathlessness just like an athlete. If I had continued to 'walk through' rehearsals, I would have been literally unfit to open. As well as the opportunity to explore the play, rehearsals also serve as training sessions, and an actor is very stupid if he doesn't take full advantage of them.

(The only time I have lost my voice – and the only time I have missed performances – was when I first joined the Old Vic Company in 1959 and found myself playing and rehearsing in classical repertory. I was not equipped for the vocal strain of playing three very different classical roles. I lost my voice, and missed two performances of *As You Like It*. Since then I have always tried to keep myself in shape.)

We were to open on a Tuesday at the Eisenhower Theatre in the Kennedy Center. We flew to Washington on the Sunday, and I started to get a bad throat. I became convinced that I couldn't speak. It was psychosomatic of course. On Monday morning I saw a doctor. He told me that I should rest my voice, and sprayed my throat with something expensive. I went to the theatre and whispered dramatically to John Dexter that I couldn't possibly rehearse. John, whose chief concern that day was with the technical aspects of the play, told me sensibly to 'go to the hotel and shut-up!'

I went to the hotel and fulfilled my fantasy of sitting with a shawl around my shoulders. I spent the whole day watching television, wrapped in a blanket, a frail old husk of forty-nine, washed out, played out, eyes watering with self-pity.

The next day I played Alceste; went to a party after the performance; and went on from there . . .

While we were in Washington, President Ford invited Diana and me to a ball at the White House. This was on a Wednesday night after we had done two performances. The company stayed behind – like children seeing mummy and daddy off in their party clothes. They also generously offered drinks and other stimulants. I was soon ready in my dinner jacket, and joined the others to await Diana's entrance. Suddenly her dresser, Bumble, mysteriously humming a song called 'The Stripper', opened her dressing-room door, and Diana strolled out clad in outrageous pink and black net underwear designed to reveal everything. This was a great success. Finally, when she was beautifully gowned and coiffured, the company saw us into a White House car and we drove off – to the sound of raucous English cheers. At the White House we were met by imposing uniformed aides and taken upstairs to wait outside the room where the ball was in progress. We were told that when the President finished dancing we would be presented. The President didn't finish dancing. He danced with his wife, with Governors' wives, and with Pearl

Bailey. We were hungry and a bit dizzy – but nobody offered us anything. After about twenty minutes we were befriended by a pretty Chinese secretary and a handsome black aide, and Diana asked them whether they could at least find us a drink. A tray laden with glasses of champagne was brought, and I think we quickly downed about half a dozen of them. Then we suggested dancing, since it didn't seem as if the President was going to leave the floor. The secretary and the aide agreed to partner us and we joined the crowded ballroom. Soon I noticed that Diana was sitting on the floor . . . but she said that she had tripped up on her new long dress. Finally I saw the President leaving the room and grabbed Diana and pulled her after him. I said we couldn't leave without a meeting. Diana was reluctant and informed a startled Senator, 'Alec's a terrible celebrity hunter!' I did all I could to get into the President's eyeline as he was bidding various people goodnight, but to no avail. After he left, we went back to the dance – which became somewhat wilder. Later that night – since we were never given any food – Diana improvised a delicious tuna-fish salad in her suite at the Watergate Hotel, and the evening ended with a lot of laughs.

To Alec McCowen
With memories of your visit to
the White House and best wishes,   Gerald R. Ford

Diana Rigg and me with President Ford

The next day there was an apology from the White House staff – 'lack of liaison' – and we were invited to a private lunch with President and Mrs Ford on the following Monday. Once again we dressed up. Once again we were collected by a White House car. On arrival we were told that unfortunately Mrs Ford was ill, but that the President might see us in the Oval Office. After a guided tour of the building, we were ushered into the famous room. When the photographers had left, we faced each other warily, and Diana and I soon realized that the President's knowledge of the theatre was minimal. However, eventually he asked us to tell him about Mrs Thatcher, and we seemed to confuse him by our preference for Shirley Williams. As he didn't make any move to dismiss us, Diana finally said: 'Well, you must be very busy . . .' and the meeting ended. Then Mrs Ford's Social Secretary took us up to the Presidential apartments and gave us a lunch consisting of chicken, bacon and tomato sandwiches and a Coca-Cola.

(By contrast, I was introduced to Senator Edward Kennedy at a party later in the week. With the full beam of the Kennedy charm, he opened the conversation by asking, 'Tell me, how do Alceste's political jokes go down with Washington audiences?' And for ten minutes he talked lucidly about the theatre. Then, he turned his attention to another guest, and I overheard him talking equally lucidly about engineering.)

Although I managed to play *The Misanthrope* with reasonable success throughout the sixteen-week American season, it was only the thought that I would never again trap myself in a prison of my own making that got me through it. I would never again demand success at the expense of health and happiness.

When the Tony Award Nominations for the best performances of the season were announced, Diana – quite rightly – was nominated for best actress. I was not nominated for best actor – although in London I had won the *Evening Standard* Award as best actor of the year in *The Misanthrope*.

The company was embarrassed.

I was not.

I was delighted.

I truthfully discovered that it didn't matter.

And this was a more important award.

It was an award of life.

My fiftieth birthday in May was the best birthday I have ever spent. The celebrations went on for days. *The Misanthrope* company gave me a party. Friends gave me parties. I spent the weekend with my friend Gil Parker at The Pines on Fire Island, and on the Sunday as we left a neighbour's house after a very generous dinner, one of our hosts yelled at us, 'Well, thanks for dropping by for seven hours!' I collapsed with laughter on the boardwalk and looked at the stars. I couldn't get up.

It didn't matter.

Back in England I decided to work as little as possible for as long as possible. This decision was helped by the fact that the National Theatre decided to put on two further short seasons of *The Misanthrope* – one in July and one in November, playing in repertory – which gave me plenty of free time.

I decided to give myself a really good fiftieth birthday present. For years I had dreamed of returning to India – where I had worked during the war, aged twenty, touring with a play called *Love in a Mist*. More specifically I dreamed of returning to Darjeeling where I had spent an enchanted holiday. There were recurring dreams about Darjeeling – which were slightly distorted. Streets, and hills, and houses, and mountains were not quite in their proper places. I kept getting lost in my dreams of Darjeeling. I kept wandering down little streets, and over fields and through thick woods, looking for the mountains. It was time to put this dream in order. I didn't believe that Darjeeling really existed. I wanted confirmation that it did.

I wanted it more than anything.

In my memory it was the most wondrous place in the world.

It was practically in heaven!

I decided to go on a Swan's Art Treasures Tour – timed to arrive in Darjeeling during the month of October when the chances of seeing the mountains are best. For most of the rest of the year the mountains are shrouded in cloud and mist, and heaven is hidden.

I was crazy with excitement.

A bizarre collection of thirty people assembled early one morning at London Airport. Americans, Dutch, French, German, Greek, and about six British. In charge of us was a splendid lady called Sybil Sassoon. She greeted me warmly by saying, 'Of course, I know your work!'

With Diana Rigg in *The Misanthrope*

We arrived in Delhi at 5.30 a.m. the following morning, where daunting hoardings warned us that 'Economic Offences Bring Stern Punishment'.

After a long wait we boarded a plane for Srinagar, which stopped en route at Amritsar.

It never left Amritsar.

We were stranded at this tiny airport.

It was like one of those old waiting-room plays or movies where groups of strangers are marooned together. It was terribly hot; the waiting-room was crowded; we were still in our English clothes; there was nothing to eat or drink; the toilets were beyond description; and amongst the party were several very old people – including an indomitable ninety-year-old American lady called Mrs Dukas. Morale was low, but Sybil suddenly galvanized us into action by ordering nine taxis and sending us off to see the famous Golden Temple of Amritsar. When we returned, battered but in better spirits, she had found us a guest house, and I shared a room – and a couple of tablets of valium – with the guest lecturer, Simon Digby.

We got to Srinagar the next day, and I was put on a house-boat called *Repose*, alone with a Mrs Kelly, who owned a drug store in North Virginia and who obviously thought she was going to be raped.

The days passed.

We spent a heavenly time in the hills at Gulmarg.

After Kashmir we went to Agra and visited the Taj Mahal.

We stayed five days in Katmandu, and I felt like a visitor from the moon.

The last part of the tour was to be Calcutta and Darjeeling; but before going to Darjeeling, this strange collection of people fascinated me more than the sight-seeing.

There was a monstrous American lady who spent half of her life doing tours, and who discovered that I was an actor. She shouted at me: 'What are you in?'

'*The Misanthrope*.'

'What?'

'*The Misanthrope*.'

She turned to her friend Ethel and yelled: 'The Missing Throat? What's that? A horror movie?'

It was the same monstrous lady who, after seeing one temple too many, remarked to Ethel within my hearing: 'This place reminds me of that Baalbeck, Lebanon. I hate that Baalbeck, Lebanon! I've been there three times and I never want to see it again!' Ethel said soothingly: 'Well we don't go there on this trip.' And the lady replied: 'Well, I hope not! But they're always trying to slip it in!'

I made friends with a delightful and witty English couple called Andrew and Polly Congreve. During our trip to Tiger Tops – a game park in Nepal – we rode on elephants through the jungle for over two hours, from the airstrip to the hotel. It was agonizingly uncomfortable. Polly Congreve observed ninety-year-old Mrs Dukas on the elephant in front of us and said: 'Isn't she wonderful!' Andrew Congreve said: 'Why?' Polly said brightly: 'Well, she hasn't complained once.' Andrew grunted: 'She's probably dead!'

Returning to Calcutta after thirty years was depressing. The city was run-down and shabby, and the poverty shocking.

The Grand Hotel was practically unrecognizable, apart from the marble floors and the palm trees in the inner court. The Metro Cinema, where in 1945 Esther Williams ran for a record season in *Bathing Beauty*, was no longer the height of air-conditioned luxury. And when I asked for Firpo's Restaurant, I was told it had closed twelve years ago.

We flew to Bagroda.

Then by car to Siliguri and started the drive up to Darjeeling. It was evening.

The Congreves let me sit in front by the driver . . .

. . . There was the little railway; surely the most wonderful railway in the world, winding wildly across the road, with the absurd little trains huffing and puffing up the immense hillside.

The sun was setting.

I was glad that I was in the front seat because my eyes were filled with sentimental tears. We moved into clouds and slowly into darkness.

We passed the happy villagers of Kurseong, and eventually, after a five-hour drive, reached Darjeeling and the Mount Everest Hotel.

There was a log fire in the bedroom, and a hot water bottle in my bed. My only worry was that I had been put in a back bedroom, and if – IF – the mountains should be visible at dawn, I might miss them. I told the Congreves of my worry (they had a front bedroom) and they promised to wake me if – IF – the miracle should happen and the mountains should appear. We were told that they hadn't been seen for a very long time.

After dinner the Congreves – who had caught something of my excitement – joined me for a walk. It was very dark, and I couldn't find a single recognizable spot. I became desperate and wanted to whimper. We walked and walked. Perhaps it had all been a dream . . . perhaps the Darjeeling of my memory had disappeared – along with the innocent twenty-year-old. Perhaps . . . We climbed a hill and seemed to be in a square. Suddenly I recognized it. I cried out with delight. 'This is the square! There's the bookshop! That's the park! That's where they tether the ponies! That's the path to the hostel! There's the main street! It's all here! It hasn't disappeared!'

The Congreves must have thought me demented. I dragged them down the main street to see if Keventers was still there. We used to drink milk and eat ice-cream in Keventers. It was there! And the Bata shoe shop! I was back! It was Darjeeling!

I couldn't sleep. I knew that my behaviour was ridiculous, but I was determined not to miss the dawn, and the Congreves might oversleep. Just before dawn, I slept. There was a bang on my door and Andrew shouted, 'MOUNTAINS!' (he sounded like someone shouting 'RABBITS!' to a dog) and I leapt out of bed.

They were there! Stretching from east to west, the huge, fantastic, white and golden, majestic range of the Himalayas, up there in the sky.

There is no other sight on earth to compare with it.

(And if there is – as the straight men say to the comics – 'I don't wish to know that!')

I put on my clothes and ran to the old walk round the hillside. It was there! It was just the same, except that it ended in a landslide.

And I'd forgotten the music in the valleys; the singing and the calls . . .

It was all there.

But what was not there was the innocent twenty-year-old. My desire to recapture myself, aged twenty, suddenly seemed indecent and undignified.

I decided to leave myself, aged twenty, alone and in peace. I would rejoice in fifty years, and look ahead.

*

I celebrated my half century in other ways.

I started a course of lessons in the Alexander Principle which turned out to be a life-saver.

I found and bought a splendid new London flat.

I decided to do an American musical.

The Alexander Principle is not easy to explain but, very briefly, it consists of a series of mental instructions to help deportment.

I needed to correct my posture. My back was curved, my shoulders were hunched, and my head was resting on the back of my neck. Shoulder muscles were tense and aching, and I had arthritic pains in my hands. In addition to growing older, this bad posture had increased while I was playing the imprisoned psychiatrist, Martin Dysart, in *Equus*. Dr Dysart was imprisoned by his job in a similar situation to my own, and to play him I had adopted – all too easily – a physically defeated, middle-aged posture.

I had mentioned the arthritic pains in my hands to my doctor: he had astonished me by saying that these pains were probably related to tension in my neck. His answer surprised me so much that I didn't question him any further on the subject, but began to think about the Alexander Principle.

An actor friend of mine called John Gray had become a pupil of Wilfred Barlow, the chief practitioner of the Alexander Principle in London. He was now a qualified teacher himself. Whenever I saw John he would nag me gently about my bad posture and tell me that I needed a course of lessons. He also said that it would help me mentally – adding intolerantly, 'More than any analyst!'

I decided to take him up on it and, before going to India, I had a two-week course of lessons with John.

It was while I was in India that I found out that it worked. We had a long drive on a dreadful bumpy road in a jeep from Darjeeling to Kalimpong, where they drink yak soup. On the way home, I was sitting in the front with our leader, Sibyl Sassoon, and I thought the journey would wreck my back – as well as my nerves and digestion. Everyone was in great discomfort. But I started to practise the Alexander Principle, and at the end of the journey I was as fresh as a daisy, and composed a new lyric to *C'est si Bon* – called 'Kalimpong' – for an amazed French couple who sat in the back seat.

The Alexander Principle helped me mentally also.

I am not tall, and it made me feel taller.

I found that even in a tense and difficult situation, it was easy to remember the basic Alexander instructions, and this made it easier to deal with the trouble. You may just as well be nervous with a relaxed neck as with a tense neck – and the relaxed neck may lead to further physical and mental relaxation.

It has also helped me professionally, and I have delighted in the novelty of occasionally being praised for the way I stand or sit. It's better than being praised for my acting.

Finding a new flat took months of searching, and I was nearly tempted to settle for something *approaching* my requirements instead of waiting for the right place. I think I found the right place. It also fulfilled the most difficult of my conditions. It was already decorated, carpeted, curtained, and half furnished. There was very little to do. I could walk in the front door and sit down. I did not have to make decisions about colour schemes, or matching fabrics, or light fixtures. Some of the flat was very unsuitably decorated – but I moved in nevertheless, and christened my pink and apple-green bedroom and bathroom 'The Debbie Reynold's Suite'.

Years of provincial repertory and touring have deadened my eyes to my immediate surroundings. There were so many drab bed-sitters; so many back-street digs; so many hotel rooms. I have lived in a hotel room for several months and not known what pictures were hanging on the wall. I love beautiful things and ugliness makes me feel physically sick, but work and friendship have always been more important than possessions and surroundings.

During *Hadrian VII* Kathleen Tynan interviewed me in my old flat with this description: 'Three walls of the sitting-room are painted army green, and the belligerent sofa is ochre yellow . . . and there is a painting of a ballet dancer with her back to us, making, I believe, as fast as she can for an exit.'

But the ballerina is still with me! She loves it!

To do an American musical was the craziest decision of my fiftieth year celebrations, and I wasted a lot of time on it – mainly because it appealed to my sense of humour.

For years I had heard tales and read tales of the dramas of

putting on a musical in America. I had grown up with countless Hollywood movies, from *Forty Second Street* onwards, where the understudy takes over from the star, and with one number creates an overnight sensation and then leaves for Acapulco with the leading man, and nobody ever seemed to do a second night or even to complete the actual show.

And I had read many biographies of brash American producers and directors, describing the hotel-room dramas in Newhaven or Philadelphia when the book is totally re-written, new numbers are composed, and somebody is always fired. (John Dexter once told me that if he ever did another American Musical he would have a clause written into his contract: 'Director Replacement Approval.')

I wanted to experience this show-business phenomenon; to have my very own tales of sleepless nights out of town, of hurriedly learnt new numbers, clashes with megalomaniac musical directors, saving the show in Boston, standing ovations on opening night, etc. . . .

In my newly found middle-aged euphoria it didn't occur to me that I could ever be the victim and not the hero of the story. And it certainly never occurred to me that such a venture could end with a whimper and not with a great big bang.

It started one night in New York when I was playing *The Misanthrope*. I was invited to a dinner party given by the veteran producer Herman Shumlin and his wife Diana. Among the guests were Melvyn Douglas, Tony Randall, and Burton Lane – the composer of *On a Clear Day*, and *Finian's Rainbow*. After a very good dinner, Burton Lane sat at the piano and started to play a selection of his music, and some of us started a competitive sing-song.

Now it so happened that I knew the score of *Finian's Rainbow* very well. In 1948 – although it sounds unlikely – and it was unlikely – I did a season of weekly repertory in St John's, Newfoundland. It was during the freezing winter months, and one of our company had the 78 records of *Finian's Rainbow*. We played them and sang to them nightly. There was nothing else to do in St John's, Newfoundland. (I cherish a postcard of St John's called simply: 'The Traffic Light, St John's, Newfoundland.)

Burton Lane and the other guests were surprised at my knowledge of the lyrics, and I finished up a winner in the singing contest with my rendering of 'When the Idle Poor become the Idle Rich'. Diana Shumlin said: 'You should do a musical!' and I said: 'I'd love to!'

Later that year Diana called me in London and told me that she had a very exciting idea. She asked if I would like to hear the score of a brand new musical which she hoped to produce. She thought that one of the leading parts would attract me.

It did. I also liked the score. But I thought the book needed some re-writing.

Then, in December – when I had finally finished playing *The Misanthrope* at the National Theatre – Diana asked me to fly to New York for a few days to meet the newly appointed director of the musical, and also to discuss the book. I agreed to do this – and also suggested that it might be a good idea if the director heard me sing. Diana ignored this.

In the worst fog for years I spent two days at Heathrow, and finally arrived in New York nearly forty-eight hours late. I rang Diana at midnight, and she invited me to lunch at Sardi's the next day to meet the director and her co-producer.

In Sardi's I was greeted with surprise by many old friends, and recklessly drank several Bull-shots.

After lunch Diana said nervously, 'They're waiting to meet you at the office.' I slurred, 'Wha' office?' and she said, 'The Frank Loesser office.' The Frank Loesser office evidently represented the author-composer-lyricist of the musical – who was working in Hollywood.

We drove off to the Frank Loesser office. I was introduced to several people, including a man they said was my accompanist. I noticed a grand piano. I noticed that it was being opened. I noticed that they were all sitting down. I noticed a score of *Finian's Rainbow* . . . I realized that it was an audition.

Diana said winsomely, 'I know you know this score backwards,' and there was a pause . . .

I excused myself and went to the lavatory. Swaying slightly from the effects of the Bull-shots, I thought: 'My agent would never allow this . . . I shouldn't do this . . . I needn't do this . . .' and then I thought: 'Oh, to hell with it! I'll do it!' and returned to the office.

I said I wouldn't do *Finian's Rainbow* but asked the accompanist to play Jerome Kern's 'I'm Old Fashioned'. I nonchalantly lit a cigarette, put my hand on the accompanist's shoulder, and started to sing.

I must have looked and sounded like the Dean Martin of Tunbridge Wells.

There was total silence when I had finished. Then the director said, 'Take it down two!' and I sang it again in a lower key.

They made slightly relieved noises, and then they asked if I could quickly learn one of the simpler numbers from the show. I boldly agreed; and ten minutes later I sang the number.

There was a lot of very audible muttering as they went into conference, and I heard one of the Frank Loesser men say, 'Well, he can sing that one. But what about the number with the high Fs? He'll never be able to do that!'

After a while Diana said: 'Wouldn't it be fun for me to record *two* numbers from the show on a cassette, and send it to the author in Hollywood as a Christmas present.' This was a blatant ploy to get me to learn the number with the high Fs.

I agreed to work with the accompanist and meet them all again two days later for the recording.

Then the director and I went off to my hotel to discuss the book. He was a splendid old man of Broadway, and obviously loved telling stories. We did little work.

Two days later the gang reassembled in the office, and we were joined by Diana's husband, Herman, who looked as if he was going to make the final decisions. He filled the office with his august presence.

I sang. Loudly. I sang the high Fs. Shakily, but loudly.

There was another silence. Then Herman said, 'Alec, you were born to do musical comedy! You've been wasting your time in straight plays! You should do musical comedy for the rest of your life!' Then he turned to the director and said, 'Why doesn't he sing it more tenderly? Doesn't he know that it's a love song?'

At some point soon after this I decided to get on to the offensive. I told them that I had no intention of doing the musical until my conditions were met. I said that as far as I was concerned the book had to be totally re-written before I would make any sort of commitment.

This was a mistake.

They were very impressed.

115

They forgot my loud voice and my lack of tenderness. They forgot my struggle to hit a high F. They assured me that the book would be re-written.

I went back to England.

Months passed.

I heard the director was fired.

I heard there was a new author.

I heard there was a completely new book.

And then I heard nothing.

Then I heard that the new book had been so bad that Diana had been taken ill.

Then I heard that there was trouble with the backers.

Then I heard that there was to be another new book.

Then I heard that there was to be not only another new book but also a completely new score and lyrics.

Then I heard that the new composer and writer wanted another star.

Diana remained loyal to me – but I thought that the time had come to call it quits. Besides, by then, I was working on a project of my own.

That was my American Musical.

While waiting for the re-writes of the musical, I did a television play. This was a first play by Christopher Wilkins called *The Late Wife*.

Then I did a stage play at the Criterion Theatre called *The Family Dance*. This was also a first play, written by Felicity Browne.

The Family Dance had an unusually good cast. Three splendid and original actresses, Annette Crosbie, Helen Lindsay and Judy Parfitt (in alphabetical order . . .) and the marvellous Michael Bryant, who played my brother. It was a very happy and funny company. We loved the play and we had a lot of laughs, but unfortunately we did not attract large audiences. Even so, we stayed at the Criterion for five months, throughout the exceptionally hot summer of 1976.

Once the play had opened I began to experience mild symptoms of that old trapped feeling again. And I had developed a strange new habit of waking up at about six o'clock every morning – no matter what time I went to sleep. There's not much to do at six o'clock in the morning.

With Annette Crosbie in *The Family Dance*

I needed a hobby.

I have always envied people with hobbies. I read, and walk, and drive, and listen to music; and occasionally I write. But I cannot make anything with my hands, or paint or draw, or play golf or tennis, or cook or even collect things.

It seemed as if my hobby would have to be my work. Sometimes during the long run of a play I have worked on a favourite Shakespearean role. Sometimes I have thought about assembling a One Man Show.

My thoughts returned to the One Man Show.

There were previous attempts.

There was a poetry recital of my own choice given one Sunday in New York during the run of *Hadrian VII*. I had enjoyed the involvement of choosing and working on the material: some Restoration poems, a Shakespeare selection, and fifteen sonnets from Meredith's great poem 'Modern Love'. It had been an exhilarating experience. They had recorded it, and I got a big thrill from listening to the loud applause and cheers at the end of the performance . . .

I had been invited to give another recital at the local open air theatre while on holiday in Kingston, Jamaica. I remembered how peaceful it was . . .

There had been a charity performance at Stagenhoe, a home for the disabled, which was being run by my sister and her husband. This was given in a large sitting-room. I remembered the feeling of power . . .

The delight of the direct contact with the audience . . .

The simplicity . . .

In 1964, during a period of doldrums, I actually wrote a One Man Show. It was a series of sketches of men, women, and children, and I called it *My Collection*. But a friend made a memorable and discouraging comment. He said: 'It's too soon for you to anthologize yourself.'

It was never done.

I have always wanted to be an entertainer rather than an actor, and idolized the great performers who can hold an audience on their own. I have already written about Jack Benny and Max Miller. But there were also the amazing seasons in the late forties when Danny Kaye entertained alone on the stage of the London Palladium. The great singers, Frank Sinatra and Judy Garland; the perfection of Miss Lena Horne.

I have got more tingling excitement from watching a great entertainer than from watching any straight actor.

Well, regretfully, I cannot sing or dance. But at least I can speak.

I thought about assembling another selection of suitable and favourite material, and was attracted to a programme of Kipling, Chesterton and Belloc. But it didn't work out.

There have been so many One Man Shows in recent years, and all the obvious material seemed to have been used.

I thought of the Bible.

Apart from recitals given by the late Charles Laughton in America, it seems to have been strangely neglected. This seemed more and more extraordinary to me.

The language of the King James Version has a personality and magic completely of its own.

I wondered how it would speak.

I had often spoken the opening of Genesis, and the great lines of Ecclesiastes . . . but these were obvious purple passages.

How would the dialogue speak?

Would it come to life like Shakespearean prose?

It is impossible to discover the vitality of Shakespearean prose just by reading it on the printed page. One needs to study it, to speak it over and over, to learn it, to discover the muscle, the colour, the wit, the complexity of the choice of words.

The King James Version was translated at the time when Shakespeare wrote his last great plays.

I began to get excited.

But what part or parts of the Bible should I choose?

My knowledge of both the Old and New Testaments was very slight. I knew that there were great stories in the Old Testament, but I didn't know where to find them.

I knew that there were great stories in the New Testament . . . Well . . .

There was 'the greatest story!'

Why had nobody ever tried to tell that?

Perhaps they had, and I had never heard of it.

I looked at the Gospels.

I had never read one of the Gospels from start to finish. I started to try. It was difficult. They just looked like a lot of formal verses on the printed page. They do not 'spring out' at one. I couldn't hear the voices . . . The very rice paper the words were printed on seemed delicate and holy, as if printed for sickly invalids.

And yet . . . Jesus seemed to be saying some strangely violent things. His behaviour seemed to be strangely provocative. There was obviously great drama there . . . if one could get it off the rice paper. If the memory of those lifeless lessons in church could be erased. If one could get away from the sing-song voices of the clergy.

I mentioned my thoughts to my sister. She had recently been getting very involved with her local church, and was obviously stimulated by practical Christianity. Her knowledge of the Bible was much greater than mine. She suggested that I study St John's Gospel.

The opening lines of St John's Gospel may be the greatest lines ever written. The mystery of the whole Gospel is overwhelming. I was overwhelmed; and knew that I did not have the perception or the intelligence to interpret it. Also it seemed to be a great essay; a study of the story of Jesus rather than the story itself. It is a study of the implications of Christ's teaching. It is a Gospel to be pondered over; to be discussed and interpreted by scholars.

I was out of my depth.

I looked at Matthew, which begins with sixteen daunting verses of genealogy. They would have to be cut.

I studied the Sermon on the Mount. It is the greatest sermon ever spoken; but it is not a story.

I was an actor and not a preacher.

It would feel presumptuous speaking the Sermon on the Mount.

And Matthew also seemed to be very long. I did not feel equipped to edit it, and didn't want to ask anyone to help me. I did not want to share my hobby with other people. The idea of a hobby is to 'do it yourself'.

I looked at Luke.

An instinct told me that it would be dangerous for me to do Luke. The style of writing is so beautiful that I would be tempted into indulgent speaking. I would fall in love with the style rather than the story. And in any case, Luke isn't really my style.

I looked at Mark.

In my ignorance I had always thought that Mark was the poor relation of the four Gospels. Most of the well-known verses of the New Testament seemed to come from Matthew, Luke or John. And because Mark is so much shorter than the other Gospels I thought that it must be the least important.

I knew nothing.

I started to read.

He certainly gets on with the story!

It may be the shortest Gospel, but it is believed to be the first Gospel.

And it is believed that it was actually related to Mark by Jesus' disciple Peter.

And if this is the case, then it is the nearest thing we have to a first-hand account of the Ministry of Jesus.

There is no account of the nativity in Mark; and very little about John the Baptist.

The writing is spare and blunt, but it moves with a wonderful speed from event to event.

It even sometimes made me laugh. But then I thought: 'That can't be right! You can't have laughs in the New Testament!'

At six o'clock in the morning, on 17 August 1976, I started to learn St Mark's Gospel – sitting up in bed in my new flat. I learnt three verses. It took about two hours.

And I continued to learn an average of three verses every morning. And it usually took two hours.

By verse 14, Mark has finished the rather formal introduction of John the Baptist and Jesus, and the story of the Ministry begins.

Jesus calls his first disciples. The pace increases. It increases with startling power for the first three chapters. It is an amazing feat of reporting.

At the end of one chapter Mark has described Jesus' entry into the synagogue; his first teaching; the disciples' astonishment; the first attack from a man with an unclean spirit; the first miracle; the domestic scene in Simon and Andrew's house; the healing of Simon's wife's mother; the first crowds; the healing of many people; Jesus' desire to pray in solitude; the disciples following him; and a miracle with a leper. By the last verse he tells us that Jesus is so popular that he has to leave town and hide in desert places.

In Chapter 2 he preaches to a crowded house in Capernaum; he heals a man sick of the palsy; he starts the confrontations with the scribes and Pharisees; he teaches by the seaside; he persuades Levi to leave his dull job and follow him; he eats and drinks with publicans and sinners; he makes jokes about it; he warns the scribes and Pharisees that there is to be a completely new doctrine; he defends his disciples for breaking the law; and he proclaims that the sabbath was made for man.

In Chapter 3 he heals a man with a withered hand and openly defies the Pharisees; they leave to plot his destruction; he returns again to the sea; multitudes follow him from all over the country; he heals many people with plagues and unclean spirits; they nearly push him into the sea; he goes up into a mountain and ordains twelve disciples; he names them; he goes into a house where the crowd is so great that they cannot eat bread; his friends say that he has gone mad; the scribes accuse him of being possessed by the devil; he warns them seriously not to blaspheme against the Holy Ghost – and the voice of the Son of God is heard for the first time. Finally his mother and his brothers call to him from outside the crowded house – presumably wanting him to come home. He defies them, and names all the believers present as his brother and sister and mother.

These three chapters take about fifteen minutes to speak.

In the words used to describe the old Western movies they are 'action-packed'.

It had been one of my fears that reciting the Gospel might be a dull exercise; that I would have to manufacture energy.

Now I had new fears. I was afraid that I wouldn't have the energy to sustain it. I was afraid that I wouldn't be able to keep up with Mark's pace. I was afraid that the speed of Mark's reporting might defeat me.

But I was also thrilled 'beyond measure'.

This was the greatest script I had ever found.

For some reason, I remember vividly certain solitary lunches during this period – on what I called St Mark days. Because once the Gospel had hooked me, I would often work on it during the day as well as early in the morning: reviewing the chapters already learnt, and reading to find out what was ahead. I started to buy books about St Mark; commentaries on St Mark; other translations of St Mark. And I would have lunch in a workman's café in Earls Court, and drink rough red wine, and I remember feeling blissfully happy.

I certainly had a hobby.

*

The construction of St Mark's Gospel is amazingly suited to the theatre. It is amazingly theatrical. It even divides itself neatly into two equal parts. Halfway through, at Chapter 9, verse 1, it reaches a great dramatic climax.

To begin with, those first three chapters establish Jesus without any possible doubt as a great hero. He is established as a teacher and healer. Mark also establishes the effect Jesus had on the people; the crowds pushing and shoving. At one point Jesus even plans with his disciples to preach from a ship away from the multitude on the shore – simply as a safety measure – 'lest they should throng him'. And the third chapter closes with the astonishing scene of Jesus' family standing outside the crowded house, sending messages to him, unable to reach him. In those three chapters he is established in theatrical terms as the leading man, the hero, the star.

Then – mercifully – Mark writes a quiet calm Chapter 4, when

Jesus just talks to the crowds, and teaches them by parables. He also carries out his plan – made in Chapter 3 – to enter into a ship and 'sit in the sea'. The pace slackens as he tries to make the crowds understand his parables. The pace slackens even more when he realizes that even his friends and disciples need to have the simplest parable repeated and explained to them. It is like talking to very young children. The chapter is a relief to both performer and audience. It is gentle and humorous and reassuring. But at the end of the chapter, with typical theatricality, Mark writes about the storm at sea and Jesus, obviously exhausted from the day's teaching, asleep on a 'pillow'; and the terror of his disciples, and the awakening of Jesus, and the stilling of the storm. The last verse contains the disciples' question: 'What manner of man is this, that even the wind and the sea obey him?'

It is the question we should all be asking.

We are a quarter of the way through the Gospel.

Another quality of the writing that thrilled me was the detailed continuity. For instance the continuity of the idea of getting into a ship for Jesus to teach from and live aboard. The actual fact of getting into the ship, Jesus asleep in the ship at the end of the day, and the eventual arrival in the ship into the country of the Gadarenes which opens Chapter 5.

I wonder what they called the ship and who was the owner.

The episode of the Gadarene swine is like a Hammer horror film. Again with theatrical construction, after the gentle quiet tone of Chapter 4, Mark tries to wake his audience up and scare them out of their wits.

It is hard for us to understand exactly what happened. The whole episode seems to be out of character for Jesus. Why should he send two thousand innocent swine to their horrible deaths of being choked in the sea? Why are the local people so frightened by the whole incident that they implore Jesus to leave their country? And why, for the only time in the whole Gospel, does Jesus instruct the healed man to tell all his friends exactly what has happened to him? It is a mysterious episode; but it is certainly very good theatre.

Having grabbed the audience by the throat, Mark then tells us of two extraordinary miracles which seem to happen at practically the same time.

With consummate narrative skill he embarks on the story of

Jairus' dying daughter – interrupts it with the story of the poor woman with the twelve-year-old issue of blood, who touches Jesus' clothes in the midst of an enormous crowd, and quietly heals herself – and then returns to the first story at the moment when we discover that Jairus' daughter is dead. The urgency of these two stories is so great, that the words come tumbling out with the speed and naturalism of a born gossip. People have actually said to me after a recital: 'Of course, you make some of it up!'

And then, with the opening of Chapter 6, we have another total change of pace, and another wonderful example of parenthetical storytelling.

Jesus comes home.

The villagers are not impressed.

'And he could there do no mighty work . . .'

And he jokes about it.

Then, with the most extraordinary and invigorating instructions, he sends his disciples out to preach and heal on their own.

And then, startlingly, Mark breaks off the story of Jesus altogether, and gives us a speciality interlude with the story of John the Baptist and Herod.

He gives the performer a breather, and he gives the audience an undemanding episode and a few laughs.

Then he returns to Jesus and the disciples with two of the most astonishing stories in the first half of the Gospel – and they are dramatically placed next to each other. The first miracle of the loaves and fishes, followed immediately by the walking on the water. These two stories are so amazing that not only is the audience stunned, but I feel that Mark himself was stunned by what he was writing. And in Chapter 6, verse 52 – for perhaps the only time in the whole Gospel – we hear the actual voice of Mark, detaching himself from the story and looking dispassionately at the disciples. The disciples are more astonished by the walking on the water than by anything else that has happened. And Mark observes wryly, 'For they considered not the miracle of the loaves: for their heart was hardened.'

Was Mark a young man? Was he better educated than the disciples? The words sound like the criticism of an educated younger man.

124

After these two amazing episodes, we reach a wonderful – but false – climax. It is as if Mark was winding up the whole story of Jesus, the teacher and healer and, with a beautifully constructed last sentence, giving us a happy ending. Everything seems to be fine. Jesus is triumphant. The crowds adore him. 'And whithersoever he entered, into villages, or cities, or country, they laid the sick in the streets, and besought him that they might touch if it were but the border of his garment: and as many as touched him were made whole.'

But we have conveniently forgotten something. And Mark never explicitly states the fact. Dramatically and theatrically he makes us discover it for ourselves.

Jesus is obviously exhausted.

And a small cloud appears on the horizon.

At the beginning of Chapter 7, the Pharisees and scribes make a carping criticism of some of the disciples. They ask Jesus why some of his disciples do not wash their hands before eating.

And Jesus starts to attack them. And it seems as if he cannot stop. He gradually widens his attack to include all the sins of mankind.

These are not the words of the fresh and happy teacher of the opening chapters, whose replies to the scribes and Pharisees were fairly brief and good humoured. This is the attack of an exhausted and impatient man. Perhaps these are the words of a man whose gift of healing has been exploited, and whose teaching is being ignored.

And then, after attacking the scribes and Pharisees, he violently attacks his disciples for their lack of understanding.

And he leaves the country.

He actually goes and hides in a house on the borders of Tyre and Sidon.

Some commentators believe that he lived there for six months.

But Mark cannot hold up his story, and almost immediately (after the bizarre episode with the Greek woman, in which Jesus says something so offensive we can only hope that it was meant as a joke) he continues on his travels, and the demands on him start again with a renewed intensity.

They beseech him to heal a deaf and dumb man. He feeds another multitude with loaves and fishes. He rebukes the Pharisees again. He seems to lose all patience with his disciples.

He fails to heal a blind man at the first attempt. He implores people over and over again not to talk about his miracles.

And then!

With the skill of a great dramatist, Mark has increased the pace. The events crowd in on one another just as they did at the beginning.

And then!

The real climax of the first half is reached.

The great moment of decision.

Jesus reveals himself as the Christ.

And he takes on himself the responsibilities of the Son of God.

And he foretells his death and resurrection.

And it seems as if this decision to reveal himself and accept the inevitability of his fate, releases the tensions that have been building up. And it seems to me that Jesus speaks with 'a new tongue'.

His tone is authoritative and confident and calm.

And he makes these uncompromising statements.

'For whosoever will save his life shall lose it; but whosoever shall lose his life for my sake and the gospel's, the same shall save it. For what shall it profit a man, if he shall gain the whole world, and lose his own soul? Or what shall a man give in exchange for his soul?'

And we finally reach the great warning. 'Whosoever therefore shall be ashamed of me and of my words in this adulterous and sinful generation; of him also shall the Son of man be ashamed, when he cometh in the glory of his Father with the holy angels.'

And we finally reach the great promise.

'Verily I say unto you, That there be some of them that stand here, which shall not taste of death, till they have seen the kingdom of God come with power.'

What does 'with power' mean? I take it to relate to the newly revealed fact of his death and resurrection. The resurrection is what will give the kingdom of God power. And many of them that stand there will certainly be living when he rises from the dead. And they will certainly realize 'the power' of Jesus, and 'the power' of God.

The second half of St Mark, after Jesus reveals himself to his disciples, and then foretells his death and resurrection, seems to have a different style, and the personality of Jesus seems to me to change.

Certain themes are emphasized.

In the first eight chapters, Mark describes eleven specific miracles of healing, as well as reporting three occasions when Jesus healed many people. There are also the two miracles of the loaves and the fishes. And there are two occasions when Jesus calms a storm at sea.

In the last eight chapters, he reports only two miracles. The emphasis is shifted to the great themes of Jesus' teaching.

The paramount importance of belief.

The warnings that the first shall be last, and the last first.

The necessity of retaining the simplicity of a child.

The exhortations to behave with compassion.

And in the first two chapters of the second half, Jesus tells his confused disciples three more times of his death and resurrection. 'But they understood not that saying, and were afraid to ask him.'

The extraordinary theatrical shape continues.

Assuming the Gospel to be in two halves, then the second half opens in much the same way as the first. There is another mystical episode; this time of the transfiguration. And as the baptism of Jesus at the beginning of the Gospel leads to a voice from heaven, saying, 'Thou art my beloved Son, in whom I am well pleased.' So the transfiguration leads to a voice coming out of the cloud, saying, 'This is my beloved Son: hear him.'

The reaction of Peter and James and John to the transfiguration and to the subsequent appearance of Elias and Moses, is wonderfully human and tongue-tied. Peter wants to build three tabernacles as a memorial to the occasion. He wants to contribute in the only way he can.

And then, as they come down from the mountain, they have a theological chat. They want to clear up the position of Elias in the order of things – presumably jealous that anyone should threaten their master Jesus as the Christ.

When Jesus joins the rest of his disciples, we are immediately involved in the story of the father of the son 'which hath a dumb spirit'. The disciples have failed to heal the boy. Jesus takes control; and the description of this miracle is longer and more complicated than any of the previous miracles.

First of all Jesus is impatient with his disciples for their failure; then he examines the boy and questions the father; the father asks, 'If thou canst do anything, have compassion on us, and help us.' Jesus gets very tough with the man, demanding 'belief'. This leads to an extraordinary outburst from the father – perhaps the only occasion in the Gospel when a supplicant remonstrates with Jesus – he 'cried out, and said with tears, Lord, I believe; help thou mine unbelief'.

And, amazingly, it seems as if Jesus still does not heal the boy.

But the man's outburst has attracted a large crowd, and 'when Jesus saw that the people came running together' he finally heals the boy. Afterwards the disciples ask him why they were not able to perform the healing and Jesus says firmly: 'This kind can come forth by nothing, but by prayer and fasting.'

This episode introduces a new emphasis on belief. Perhaps Jesus will no longer indiscriminately perform miracles; perhaps he has decided that his teaching is more important. Certainly this is a different personality to the exuberant young man who 'healed many' in the early chapters of the Gospel.

And now it seems as if Jesus concentrates his attention on his disciples. He has to prepare them. They 'passed through Galilee; and he would not that any man should know it. For he taught his disciples . . .' How did they pass through Galilee without any man knowing it? Perhaps they travelled at night. Perhaps they travelled off the beaten track across country.

When they reach Capernaum there is a beautiful domestic scene between Jesus and the disciples. I picture these tired and dusty men at the end of a long day's walking, in the privacy of a family home, presumably the guests of a large family. Perhaps it is the house of Simon and Andrew. During the journey Jesus has overheard the disciples discussing among themselves 'who should be the greatest'. And this leads to the introduction of the revolutionary Christian theme, 'If any man desire to be first, the same shall be last of all, and servant of all.' And Jesus illustrates this theme with a child of the household, and throughout the discussion that follows, one must remember the child in Jesus' arms.

The belief of a child, is the true uncomplicated belief. The child is the guideline.

For a long time I could not understand the seemingly savage instructions of Jesus about cutting off offending arms and legs, and plucking out offending eyes, with the alternative of hell-fire, until I remembered that the child is presumably still in his arms. Then, instead of this being a terrifying Old Testament tirade, the passage becomes a matter of simple choices. I take it that the offending members are our friends and relatives, and if they become our enemies then we sever our connections with them. And this lesson springs initially from the horrifying thought of anyone offending the child in Jesus' arms.

The wonderful scene ends with what seems to be a benediction of the child and the disciples. 'Have peace one with another.' It is so simple.

The travelling continues. They arrive 'into the coasts of Judaea by the farther side of Jordan' (wherever that may be) and after a trick question from the Pharisees about divorce, which Jesus answers unequivocally, there is another episode with children.

The disciples make the awful mistake of keeping children from Jesus. And in the succinct words of the King James Version 'he was much displeased'. And, again, he explains the precious qualities of a child. 'Whosoever shall not receive the kingdom of God as a little child, he shall not enter therein.'

This surely doesn't mean that one has to *be* a child to enter into the kingdom of God – but that as adults we should retain the open-mindedness, the receptivity, the wonder, the joy, the simplicity, the candour and the eagerness of a child.

It seems as if Jesus is now using the ordinary events of the day to teach his disciples. They certainly always had a difficult time with the parables.

The next incident is the wonderfully good-humoured encounter with the rich young man. He comes running up to Jesus in the road, kneels to him, and asks him straight out: 'Good Master, what shall I do that I may inherit eternal life?' I think that Jesus is startled by the innocent urgency of the huge question. First of all he reprimands the young man for his flattery, and then he asks him if he knows the basic commandments. And again the answer comes with delicious naïvety: 'Master, all these have I observed from my youth.' I think he amuses Jesus – in the way one is amused when one can't quite believe one's ears. Mark says: 'Then Jesus beholding him loved him.' I imagine Jesus trying to look at the young man, and turning away and laughing. And he teases the perfect young man with: 'One thing thou lackest: go thy way, sell whatsoever thou hast, and give to the poor, and thou shalt have treasure in heaven'; and then challenges him with: 'and come, take up the cross, and follow me'. And with superb understatement Mark says: 'And he was sad at that saying, and went away grieved: for he had great possessions.' The encounter provokes a lively discussion about wealth between Jesus and the disciples, and it leads once again to the startling teaching: 'But many that are first shall be last; and the last first.'

We are suddenly informed that 'they were in the way going up to Jerusalem'. And from now on Mark repeats the name of the city with great dramatic effect. We realize that the final challenge to the establishment is going to be made. And Jesus seems eager to meet the challenge. With total disregard to his safety 'Jesus went before them: and they were amazed; and as they followed, they were afraid'. And again he tries to comfort them as he foretells his own death and resurrection.

It is perhaps the sudden proximity of Jerusalem that gives James and John the courage to make their very understandable request for preferential treatment in heaven. 'Grant unto us that we may sit, one on thy right hand, and the other on thy left hand, in thy glory' – which is soon equally understandably followed by: 'And when the ten heard it, they began to be much displeased with James and John.'

Even after all the teaching, all the experiences, the close relationship with Jesus, the disciples – even the favourite disciples – retain their human frailty. And even after the two quite recent occasions when Jesus has taught that the 'first shall be last; and the last first' they fall into the trap of expecting worldly order again. Was Jesus exasperated or depressed? Was he, even amongst the twelve, a very lonely man? Maybe. But he teaches them yet again: 'whosoever will be great among you, shall be your minister: And whosoever of you will be the chiefest, shall be servant of all'.

How many times must it be said?

The journey continues, and as they leave Jericho there is the last recorded miracle of healing. The very moving story of blind Bartimaeus, who shouts out from the highway side to catch Jesus' attention as the huge crowd passes by. The demand for mercy is blunt and crude, but the event is told with great dignity as if it was the story of a king rather than a beggar. When the crowd tells Bartimaeus that Jesus will see him, there is the wonderfully constructed verse: 'And he, casting away his garment, rose, and came to Jesus.' And the pace and excitement of the Gospel suddenly increase as Mark writes: 'And immediately he received his sight, and followed Jesus in the way. *And when they came nigh to Jerusalem . . .*'

Now the disciples find the colt 'whereon never man sat' and 'cast their garments on him; and he sat upon him' and there is the great procession, and the cries of: 'Hosanna in the highest. *And Jesus entered into Jerusalem.*'

This is a great climax, but typically the storyteller immediately disarms us. Instead of following this up with a scene of action, Mark simply writes that 'when he had looked round about upon all things, and now the eventide was come, he went out unto Bethany with the twelve'.

Instead of the great confrontation that we might have expected, we now get the most trivial story in the Gospel. Instead of a portrait of the Son of Man in the great city, Mark gives us the story of a hungry and probably nervous man getting no breakfast and outrageously cursing a fig tree for bearing no figs. And with a wealth of unspoken comment, Mark writes: 'And his disciples heard it.'

But is this really a trivial and unimportant story?

To me it seems wonderful to be reminded at this stage that Jesus speaks and feels exactly like one of us. It is wonderful to be reminded before the great events that follow that Jesus was an ordinary man. Already Mark has described him tired and sleeping. There have been scenes with him impatient and exasperated. Now we see him hungry and childish.

'*And they come to Jerusalem:*' and, on an empty stomach, Jesus 'began to cast out them that sold and bought in the temple, and overthrew the tables of the moneychangers, and the seats of them that sold doves' and he openly attacks the chief priests for making the temple 'a den of thieves'.

Can we imagine such a thing happening today in St Peter's or St Paul's or Notre Dame? No wonder that the chief priests 'sought how they might destroy him: for they feared him', and no wonder that 'all the people was astonished at his doctrine'.

But Mark doesn't linger over this. Like an experienced comedy writer he takes us back to the fig tree. 'And in the morning, as they passed by, they saw the fig tree dried up from the roots.' And Peter, who obviously recalled this incident very clearly, decides to draw Jesus' attention to it. Is there an edge of malice to: 'Master, behold the fig tree which thou cursedst is withered away'? Is there a suppressed smile? Are the disciples amused that their paragon has behaved in such a petulant way? If so, the malice, the smile and the amusement are short-lived. 'And Jesus answering saith unto them [not 'And Jesus said unto them;' not 'And Jesus answered and said unto them'; but the weightier, 'And Jesus answering saith unto them.'], HAVE FAITH IN GOD.' And the incident is suddenly transformed into one of the greatest lessons of faith and belief in the New Testament.

This is followed by the instruction to forgive 'if ye have aught against any'. At first I couldn't see the connection between the great lecture on faith and belief and this instruction to forgive, until I wondered if it could possibly relate to the fig tree. I hope it does.

'And they come again to Jerusalem . . .'

Now Mark sets the scene in the temple. Without any more interruptions he reports at least nine wonderful stories of Jesus in the temple.

Stories in which Jesus unmistakably writes his own death sentence.

He tricks and rebuffs the chief priests and the scribes and the elders, by demanding recognition of John the Baptist.

He tells the parable of the vineyard, giving warning that God will destroy his enemies.

He gleefully recalls the wonderful scripture: 'The stone which the builders rejected is become the head of the corner.'

He routs the Pharisees and the Herodians with their trick question about Caesar.

He mocks the Sadducees with their elaborate question about resurrection.

He tells the 'discreet' scribe that the two most important commandments are to love God, and to 'love thy neighbour as thyself'.

He contradicts the scribes who say that: 'Christ is the son of David' – and here Mark writes the most adorable line: 'And the common people heard him gladly.'

He savagely mocks and denounces the scribes for their hypocrisy.

And, finally, he watches the poor widow throw her two mites into the treasury, and praises her contribution above all others.

'For all they did cast in of their abundance; but she of her want did cast in all that she had, even all her living.'

And as he goes out of the temple, one of his disciples looks back and, it seems to me, begs Jesus to at least pay some respect to the great buildings. And we hear the ruthless and awesome reply: 'there shall not be left one stone upon another, that shall not be thrown down'.

Imagine the effect of all this on the disciples. Imagine them watching him and listening to him in the temple. Imagine their wonder at his audacity. Imagine their fear for his safety. Imagine their excitement.

Imagine them, in Chapter 13, begging him to share his great knowledge with them. Or at least imagine Peter and James and John and Andrew, because the others, as so often before, seem to have got left out.

They sit upon the Mount of Olives and beg Jesus to: 'Tell us, when shall these things be? and what shall be the sign when all these things shall be fulfilled?'

And Jesus makes the longest speech in St Mark's Gospel. He does not directly answer their question, but with many extraordinary prophecies; and with the extraordinary promise that they shall 'see the Son of man coming in the clouds with great power and glory'; and with the comfort that 'then shall he send his angels, and shall gather together his elect from the four winds, from the uttermost part of the earth to the uttermost part of heaven'; he finally commands them and us to 'watch'.

This speech also contains the most confident statement ever made by a man: 'Heaven and earth shall pass away: but my words shall not pass away.' Perhaps followed at a distance by Shakespeare's: 'Not marble, nor the gilded monuments of princes, shall outlive this powerful rime.'

Mark has constructed his Gospel with the skill of a great dramatist. The events of a great tragic play lead us inexorably to the final catastrophe. We know the end is inevitable. And there is the acceptance of destiny which sets the protagonist above the rest of mankind. Lear's harsh statement of fact: 'I am bound upon a wheel of fire, that mine own tears do scald like molten lead.' Or Hamlet's limpid invitation: 'If it be now, 'tis not to come; if it be not to come, it will be now; if it be not now, yet it will come: the readiness is all.'

In the great speech on the Mount of Olives, Jesus helps his

disciples to prepare for the years ahead. He warns them that the pain and hardship of life will continue. He speaks of horror and afflictions. He asks them to 'endure unto the end'.

And with this speech, his ministry has almost ended. His work is almost done. Mark warns us that the chief priests and the scribes are waiting to seize him and put him to death.

But then he surprises us again. In the same way that the entry into Jerusalem is interrupted with the human story of the fig tree, so the betrayal of Jesus is interrupted by another human story. 'In the house of Simon the leper, as he sat at meat' a woman recklessly pours a box of expensive ointment on Jesus' head. And this little story provides us with a last reminder of the importance of compassion.

Already, in the second half of the Gospel, Jesus has told his disciples: 'He that is not against us is on our part,' and 'Whosoever shall give you a cup of water to drink in my name . . . he shall not lose his reward.' We have been told the compassionate story of the poor woman with her gift of two mites. Now we are told the equally compassionate story of a rich woman with her gift of three hundred pence worth of ointment – 'very precious'.

'And they murmured against her.' And in wonderfully simple words Jesus attacks the murmurers with: 'Let her alone; why trouble ye her? she hath wrought a good work on me.' And he continues to attack them; and there is the comforting line: 'She hath done what she could': and finally Jesus predicts that her action will be spoken of for as long as the Gospel is preached.

In St Matthew's Gospel, the chief murmurer against the woman is identified as Judas Iscariot. It would seem as if Jesus' defence of the rich woman is too much for Judas to bear, and he goes straight to the chief priests to betray his Master.

I had always thought of Judas, in theatrical terms, as being a straightforward villain. But, perhaps, on the evidence of the story of the rich woman and the ointment, Judas is a much more complicated character. Perhaps he regarded himself as a more religious man than Jesus. Perhaps he was a 'holy Joe'. Perhaps the unconventional behaviour of Jesus gradually proved too much for him. Perhaps Jesus' statement about the woman with the ointment; 'Wheresoever this gospel shall be preached throughout the whole world, this also that she hath done shall be spoken of for a memorial of her', finally convinced him that

Jesus was nothing more than an irreligious megalomaniac.

I have a feeling of somebody 'holier than thou'. There is a whiff of the religious intolerance of the Inquisition.

In any case, this little domestic scene precipitates the departure of Judas from the twelve, and the arrest, the trial and the crucifixion of Jesus.

In the last three chapters of the Gospel, Mark writes simply and movingly of these events; but just occasionally he introduces what seem to be irrelevant details. And yet, it is these seemingly irrelevant details that give the Gospel the ring of truth.

And we are very aware of the voice of Peter.

Surely only Peter would remember that when Jesus wakes him in Gethsemane, he called him by his original name of Simon. 'Simon, sleepest thou? couldest not thou watch one hour?' Only Peter would recall that, when he followed Jesus afar off into the palace of the High Priest, he 'warmed himself at the fire'. Only Peter would have confessed that after he had denied all knowledge of Jesus – not once but three times – 'he wept'.

Then there are the unexpected details about new characters. The man who carried the cross: 'one Simon a Cyrenian, who passed by, coming out of the country, the father of Alexander and Rufus'.

The woman with Mary Magdalene who was 'looking on afar off' called 'Mary the mother of James the less and of Joses, and Salome; (who also, when he was in Galilee, followed him, and ministered unto him)'.

The man who laid the body of Jesus in the sepulchre: 'Joseph of Arimathaea, an honourable counsellor, which also waited for the kingdom of God.'

Perhaps these people became close friends of the disciples, and this is why these details are so faithfully recorded.

But there is one new character who is unnamed. He is the most intriguing of them all. When Jesus is arrested, 'there followed him a certain young man, having a linen cloth cast about his naked body; and the young men laid hold on him: and he left the linen cloth, and fled from them naked'.

It is thought that this young man might have been Mark.

At first I dismissed this as a fanciful idea, but gradually I have come to believe it. Why on earth should the incident be recorded by Mark after nearly forty years. Isn't it possible that the young Mark had heard Jesus teach in the temple? Isn't it possible that

135

he loved Jesus? Isn't it possible that from his home he heard Judas and the soldiers on their way to the Mount of Olives? Wouldn't it be natural for him to rush from his bed to warn Jesus of their arrival? And wouldn't it be natural for him to record the incident? To record his own eye-witness account of the arrest of Jesus? And indeed to record his own small indignity?

I hope so. The modesty of the description seems to be typical of Mark. And the seemingly irrelevant details of the new characters in these last chapters, would mean that Mark actually knew these people.

Now there is something else.

And it is the whole point of the Gospel.

It is belief in the resurrection.

When I compared St Mark's Gospel with the great tragedies of the theatre, it was a stupid comparison. St Mark's Gospel is not a play. And it is certainly not a tragedy.

And whether or not you and I believe in God, and whether or not you and I believe in the resurrection, the glory of the Gospel is that Jesus believes in God, and that Jesus believes in the resurrection.

There is a sentence spoken by Jesus after the Last Supper: 'I will drink no more of the fruit of the vine, until that day that I drink it new in the kingdom of God.'

To me this is the most joyful sentence ever spoken by a man. This is a confirmation of total belief, expressed in a way that everyone can understand.

The confidence of this vow transforms the ensuing tragedy of the crucifixion into something which is only a preparation for the coming of the kingdom of God WITH POWER.

The growth and survival of Christianity is an astonishing thing, when one considers that even the contemporaries of Christ did not believe in his resurrection. But by some miracle, the events of Jesus' life and death were written down. His teaching was recorded. His faith was so great that nearly forty years after his death, Mark wrote his Gospel. And soon the others followed.

And Gospel means good news.

This little commentary on St Mark's Gospel is an actor's

commentary. I have made observations of character, and written about scenes and situations, in the same way that I would study a script. I have looked for what is unusual and unexpected. I have lingered over whatever seems to be especially colourful or eccentric. I have searched for the personality of the writer. It is a brief and superficial examination of a story which has inspired men for nearly two thousand years. But perhaps my ignorant enthusiasm may illuminate a few aspects of the story which are taken for granted by believers. Perhaps, by shining my crude actor's torch on these great events, some of them are seen in a new light. And I hope, one day, that I shall write a fuller account of my unexpected middle-aged encounter with St Mark.

*

I was able to work on the first half of St Mark for about six months. The West End play, *The Family Dance*, finished its run, and the only major interruption was a television production of Noël Coward's *Private Lives* in which I played Elyot opposite Penelope Keith's Amanda.

Playing opposite Penelope Keith in *Private Lives*

We tremulously sang 'Someday I'll find You', and we wrestled on expensive rugs. She broke a gramophone record over my head, and I spanked her silk clad bottom.

Then I went back to the Gospel.

By January, I knew roughly eight chapters – or, perhaps, eight chapters roughly.

Then I went to New York to play my original role in *Equus* for a four-week season – I stayed for nine weeks. And did no study at all. It's hard to study in New York.

With Dorothy Tutin in *Antony and Cleopatra*

When I came home my memory had faded, and I had to start at the beginning of the Gospel again. I slowly revised the first half – and learnt two more chapters.

Then I had to stop again.

In a moment of rashness, I had agreed to join the Prospect Theatre Company and play Antony in *Antony and Cleopatra*.

It was a distinguished cast. Dorothy Tutin was my Cleopatra, Timothy West was Enobarbus, and Derek Jacobi played Octavius Caesar.

I had always thought that *Antony and Cleopatra* was my favourite play, and had often idly thought of playing Antony. You fall in love with certain roles when you are young, and you never really get over it. At least, you never get over it unless you get the chance to work it out of your system. You need to play the part – to discover what a bastard it can be.

A dream was fulfilled when I was thirty-four of playing Richard II at the Old Vic. This was a moderately successful attempt – but I had not realized the richly and rigidly poetic style of the writing. It was hard to find the human being under the formal forest of verse, and my schoolboy crush on Richard was cured.

I have always adored Hotspur, and had a strong impression in my mind of how he should look and sound. Now I am too old for Hotspur.

But Antony was fifty-two when he met Cleopatra.

It was my own age at the time.

And Antony has a Gemini-like quality of forgetfulness akin to treachery, which I understand very well. And the romantic death-wish. And the great Shakespearean imagery. And the challenge of an undoubted heavyweight. (Hamlet is a middle-weight by comparison.)

There is a story of the great cricketer Sir Leonard Hutton. He was asked by a group of experts why he had failed with a certain ball. Polite and complicated theories were advanced to lessen the embarrassment of the lapse. But finally Sir Leonard simply said: 'I missed it!'

I missed it with Antony.

When I played Richard II at the Old Vic in 1960, there was a headline over a review in a newspaper: 'He is too short to play a king.' It was very hurtful. Despite the Alexander Principle, I never felt tall enough for Antony.

I strutted.

In 1952 I had been a member of the Laurence Olivier-Vivien Leigh *Antony and Cleopatra* company in New York. I could never forget the echoes of Olivier's great trumpeting voice.

I bellowed.

Also, it was not a good production. The politics of the play were emphasized, but not the romance; not the huge, crumbling, ridiculous romance of two middle-aged people refusing to face reality.

And we developed a stupid theory during rehearsals that Antony and Cleopatra should never make love in public, so we always tried to keep a physical distance between each other. We thought it would be better if the audience imagined how passionately we made love in private. In the play, Antony and Cleopatra are never seen in private – except to quarrel violently – and it obviously appeared to the audience that we couldn't stand the sight of each other.

In addition to all of this, the company loathed the costumes and the scenery.

We played eight performances at the Old Vic and then went on a wildly eccentric tour playing in repertory with *Hamlet*, a production called *War Music*, and later with Dryden's *All for Love*. Touring these four productions proved to be so expensive that all the scenery was discarded in the middle of the tour – which was probably a slight improvement.

The first performance of *Antony and Cleopatra* on tour was in a semi open-air theatre in Ljublana, Yugoslavia. It rained, and the theatre was only about a sixth full.

The next performance was in the open air in Dubrovnik. We played in front of a palace, and the noise of birds attracted to the stage lights, and the music of a neighbouring café orchestra, made us almost totally inaudible.

The third performance was in a very impractical open-air location in Split, Yugoslavia. As the adjoining open-air restaurant refused to close until the performance started, it was very difficult to rehearse. We could not find our way from one side of the stage to the other, as it involved going down several back alleys and round a back street. Indeed one of the girls, acting as a dresser, was attacked by local youths as she searched in vain for her actor.

We then flew to Jordan and gave a gala performance for the King in a mammoth auditorium in Amman. For reasons of security, only the King's guests were admitted – and the theatre was about a tenth full. Soldiers with machine-guns walked around backstage, and became very nervous every time a sword was drawn. The King wisely left the theatre after the performance without meeting us. He obviously had troubles of his own.

The wear and tear of these four eccentric dates was damaging to an already flawed production – to say nothing of the wear and tear on the costumes. These now started to fall apart. Fungus grew in the armour.

We were the chief dramatic attraction of the 1977 Edinburgh Festival, and we played at the Assembly Hall. The production had to be re-staged for the fifth time.

At best my performance was described as 'courageous'.

Also, I became accustomed to an unusual accolade from friends who saw the production. During the scene on Pompey's ship, I did an abandoned, drunken dance. Friends would come backstage and invariably the first thing they would say was: 'I loved your dance!' – I must be the only Antony chiefly praised for his dancing.

While in Edinburgh, I involved myself in a staged Sunday reading of *Paradise Lost*, playing Satan. I hoped to find my form again. But an Edinburgh critic gave me the worst notice of my life – referring to my 'ludicrous posturings'.

It was very low ebb.

The Monday after *Paradise Lost* – after I had read the frightful notice – I forced myself to go into town and have a good meal. Such is my conceit, that I thought that there would be pointed fingers and whisperings of accusation against the despoiler of Milton and the inadequate Antony.

And, instead, two very strange things happened.

Months before I had told a story by H. G. Wells on television. This had been spoken directly into the camera, and took about forty minutes. It was an experiment – which must have proved too simple to be of interest to the planners of programmes. When I saw it, I thought it was the best thing that I had ever done; but it was not reviewed, and hardly anybody else seemed to have seen it. Nobody spoke of it.

Walking down Castle Hill on that bloody Monday, a lady suddenly stopped me in the street and told me how much she had enjoyed the story on TV.

Then I went for a drink in a little bar, and the young Scots barman behaved as if Jack Nicholson had walked in. His enthusiasm was entirely caused by the television story. Neither of these two people knew anything about Antony, nor about anything else I had done.

I, of course, immediately related this praise for my story-telling to St Mark, and hoped that it was a good sign.

And that evening, I saw the wonderful Julie Harris, doing her

Solo Performance about Emily Dickinson at the Lyceum Theatre. She was sensationally good. I went backstage and hugged her. She didn't know why I hugged her so hard.

The Prospect tour continued.

We played in Birmingham – where I gave one good performance when I 'didn't care'. But those 'don't care' performances are very rare, and not to be depended on . . .

We played in Sunderland, Norwich, Cardiff, Wolverhampton, Manchester, Leeds and Newcastle, and then returned to the Old Vic for a month.

Meanwhile – as they say in the serials – back in the hotel rooms I had been quietly studying St Mark.

One of the attractions of the Prospect job was that it gave me plenty of free time to concentrate on the Gospel; and, unknown to the company, I was learning parables in Ljublana, and confronting scribes and Pharisees in Split. I studied the Last Supper in Norwich, and reached the resurrection in Manchester.

*

Many people are amazed that actors can learn lines. It seems to be a great mystery. 'How do you learn your lines?' they ask, as if there was a secret formula. To me it is far more surprising that a musician can learn all those notes; that an engineer can understand the parts of an engine; that a doctor can diagnose all those symptoms; that a good taxi-driver can memorize all the streets in London. To me it is much more impressive that students of law and of medicine spend years learning the basics of their professions; that an architect can design a church, a factory or a hotel; and, perhaps most impressive of all, that a bridge-builder can construct a bridge.

Learning lines is donkey work. There is no secret formula. You sit or stand or walk and – learn your lines. Some actors like to have their lines heard by other people; some actors use a tape-recorder; but most actors take the script, and with a card or envelope or even their hand, they go down the page, over and over and over again, slowly driving the lines into their heads. I suppose, described in this way, it is a bit impressive. But to an actor it is not impressive – it is very, very boring . . . and it is something that just has to be done, or else you cannot work.

Learning St Mark took me sixteen months and, for the most

part, was a great pleasure. It was a pleasure because, as I have already written, until I *learnt* the lines, I didn't fully understand them. Until I was forced to examine each sentence with the utmost care, I didn't understand the choice of words or the construction.

At first, for instance, I was depressed by the continual repetition of 'He said unto them' or 'He answered and said unto them' or 'And Jesus answering saith unto them', until I realized that there was a pattern to the choice of these phrases; and that Mark used the first phrase in an ordinary exchange, the second phrase if Jesus was making a particular point, and the last phrase is usually spoken when Jesus completely routs his questioners. Then, later, I discovered a further reason to love the constant repetition of these prosaic phrases, and to gather enormous energy from them.

Learning St Mark was a revelation. A revelation of an extraordinary man; of extraordinary events; of extraordinary hope. And learning St Mark in the King James Version revealed a blunt and direct, almost naïve style, which is sometimes consciously humorous, and often impressively particular in detail. Whether or not you are 'a believer', it is impossible to study St Mark carefully and not *know* – without any shadow of doubt – that something amazing happened in Galilee two thousand years ago.

Looking back on those months of learning, I remember my cynicism as I started each new, and seemingly lifeless chapter, convinced that it would continue to be dull or incomprehensible to me, and that I would lose my enthusiasm for the whole project and give up. But apart from a testing time with Chapter 7 – when several verses resisted me stubbornly for many days – learning St Mark was a joy.

The most difficult part of an actor's job is not *learning* his lines, but to bring his lines to life; to compel an audience to listen to him and to watch him; to hold their attention; to involve them; to *entertain* them.

With St Mark, for the first time, I was determined to be my own director. This would mean that I was not only responsible for the interpretation of the text, but also for the presentation of the Gospel on a stage.

How should it be done?

At first, my only idea was to come on stage and, as I spoke the first lines, to take off my jacket and roll up my sleeves. This was an instinctive feeling – to present a man starting work. I practised this simple activity many times in my living-room – and always wondered what I should do with my jacket once I had taken it off. It would look ridiculous to hang it on a hook . . . Then I thought that I would not want to stand up throughout the entire recital, so I decided to have a chair on stage. I could drape my jacket on the back of the chair.

Then, one day, when I grew hoarse with rehearsing, I realized that it would be necessary to have a jug of water and a glass on stage. They would have to stand on something. I considered copying the brilliant comedian Dave Allen who uses a combined stool and tray. Then I decided on a table or desk.

At the same time I was wondering about the character of St Mark. Should I try to *be* St Mark? Who was Mark? What was he doing? Reporting . . . Should I play Mark as a reporter – entering like the cliché Hollywood reporter wearing a hat and a mackintosh – dictating to a secretary – dictating into a recorder . . .?

This soon seemed unnecessarily gimmicky.

I decided that I would simply enter with my copy of St Mark, put it on the table, take off my jacket and tell the story – as if it had just been told to me.

I wondered, who was my audience? Were they friends? Were they enemies? Were they cynics or were they sympathetic? It made a great difference to the telling of the story. I practised with various imaginary audiences. As I rehearsed in my living-room, I sometimes made dummies and placed them on the sofa facing me. Dummies made with coats and hats – large photographs of friends and acquaintances . . . sometimes, a very surprised old teddy bear watched me . . .

Soon the living-room of my London home became too cramped and small and, whenever I could, I went down to Sandgate in Kent, where I am part owner of a rambling garden flat. This flat is in a grey brick Victorian house, halfway up a cliff, and it has a large living-room. It was in this living-room, with the furniture stacked up against the walls, that I worked out my movements in St Mark. I would drive down to the coast, stock up with food and drink from the large supermarket in Folkestone, and rehearse alone, at all hours of the day and night.

The minimum furniture I needed for the presentation soon became a table and three chairs. The first chapter was simply direct story-telling. Then, in Chapter 2, I started to move about, and suddenly the table and three chairs became the interior of a house. When I moved in front of the table and chairs, I was in the street or by the sea. When I moved behind them, I was in the mountains. When the house was crowded with people, the scribes and Pharisees sat on the right near the door. Once I had established this in my mind, I had no need to be imaginative; the story started to push me around. The table and chairs started to represent other things. The ship from which Jesus tells the parables. The bedroom where Jairus's daughter lies dead. The dining-room of Herod's birthday. The temple in Jerusalem.

In the early days of rehearsal, I inevitably fell into the trap of making Jesus sound 'holy' and 'self-righteous'. This is a well-intentioned error which has led many professional actors astray – to say nothing of the clergy and readers of lessons in churches. It seems proper to be devout and respectful when speaking the words of Christ; but this usually leads to a lifeless and solemn interpretation, making Jesus sound remote and wishy-washy.

At the end of Chapter 1, Jesus cures a leper. The leper challenges Jesus with great energy: '"If thou wilt, thou canst make me clean." And Jesus, moved with compassion, put forth his hand, and touched him, and saith unto him, "I will; be thou clean."' At first, my instinct was to describe the compassion of Jesus, and the line came out in a sickly sentimental way. Then, linking the challenge of the leper's, 'If thou wilt', with Jesus', 'I will', I realized that in reality Jesus would be assuring the leper with the utmost strength. 'I will', would be spoken with confidence and joy. 'Be thou clean', would be an unanswerable order. The miracle would be inevitable.

It is very easy to make Jesus sound long-suffering – especially with the disciples – but this produces an unpleasantly martyred tone. After the first, very simple parable of the sower and the seed, Jesus is asked by friends and disciples to explain it again. Jesus says: 'Know ye not this parable? and how then will ye know all parables?' If this is said sadly or patiently, Jesus sounds like a prig. It is surely spoken with astonished, healthy sarcasm.

When Jesus decides to feed five thousand men in a desert place, and calmly asks his disciples: 'How many loaves have ye?' he adds the tiny line, 'Go and see.' I doubt if Jesus said this

patiently. I imagine the disciples looking at him in total disbelief
– probably about to answer back derisively – and Jesus shouting
at them: 'GO AND SEE.'

There is no sign of 'Gentle Jesus, meek and mild' in St Mark's
Gospel.

For a long time I considered the voice of Jesus and the sound
of Jesus. With a play, this is something that usually emerges in
rehearsal; it is not something that I would think about in an
analytical way. The voice of a character usually dictates itself by
his actions and intentions. But St Mark's Gospel is not a play.
And I was not acting the role of Jesus. I was trying to tell the
story of Jesus. But even a storyteller often colours his voice to
indicate the personality of his characters. Some storytellers even
do lifelike impersonations.

I considered giving Jesus and his disciples country accents.

There is a verse in Chapter 14, when Peter is accused by the
servants of the high priest of knowing Jesus. They say: 'Surely
thou art one of them: for thou art a Galilaean, and *thy speech
agreeth thereto.*'

It always helps me, when studying a script, to understand the
geography of the setting. If a scene takes place in a room, I am
always absolutely clear about the shape and description of the
fourth wall; and I like to know exactly where the room is in
relation to the rest of the house. Then I will picture the street
outside, and the surrounding town or country. This
geographical obsession is not something that shows itself to an
audience; but it helps me privately to concentrate. While
studying St Mark, I was greatly helped by little maps of Palestine
at the time of Christ, and knowing the position of Galilee or
Nazareth or Capernaum in relation to Jerusalem. I was
surprised to find that even the 'borders of Tyre and Sidon' –
which sound so far away – are relatively near; and that the
distances travelled by Jesus might be contained in Kent and
Sussex.

I considered giving Jesus and the disciples a Kentish accent –
such as I had myself when I was a schoolboy. I thought it might
emphasize the drama of this group of countrymen and
fishermen going to the big city. Whenever Jerusalem is mentioned in the Gospel, it has the glamorous sound of London
or New York to a country boy today. I also thought that it would
help to colour my performance.

I practised the Kentish accent, but it was very ugly.

I practised other accents, but they soon sounded ridiculous.

The only reasonable possibility was to go far north. For a week or so, Jesus and his disciples were Scottish.

Then I stopped this nonsense.

It was a lack of faith.

Fellow actors will recognize the symptoms. There is often a time in rehearsals when a production and performances get into the doldrums. This is the time when actors will say during a coffee break, 'Why don't we do this as a musical!' And terrible songs are invented, with titles made from the worst lines in the script. Or someone will say 'Why don't we make them all gay!' And a great deal of outrageous 'camping about' ensues. This is a time when you are not yet equipped to give a fleshed-out performance, and panic sets in. Eventually you usually go back to your first intentions.

I went back to my first intentions with St Mark – to tell the story in the simplest possible way. This was partly through my own instincts, but also because I had a welcome confirmation of my intentions from someone I respected.

Very few people knew that I was working on St Mark. I didn't want to risk discouraging reactions.

My friend Geoffrey Burridge knew, and used to refer to it as my 'drawings'. 'Are you doing your drawings?' he would ask whenever he wanted to know whether I was busy.

My mother and sister knew, and were very encouraging.

And, early on, I told my friend and agent, Larry Dalzell. He was, as ever, loyally enthusiastic.

But after nine months' work I needed further confirmation that I was working on a practical idea.

I decided to ask the writer and director Ronald Eyre for his opinion. He is an old acquaintance – and I am always hoping that one day we will work on something together. It so happened that when we met at this time, in April 1977, Ron had been working for three years on an astonishing religious project of his own; a project which made a recital of St Mark seem positively puny. He had conceived his thirteen-part television series called *The Long Search* – which was nothing less than an examination of the chief religions of the world. He had already finished the filming, and was now busy editing and writing. Understandably, he was as exhilarated about *The Long Search* as I was about St Mark, and we spent an exceptionally good-mannered evening giving each other turns to speak. I was delighted by his immediate reaction when I first told him of my plan to recite St Mark. He said, 'Yes! I think you should simply come on stage as if to say "Listen! A man just told me this!" As if you were telling the story for the very first time.' He confirmed that Mark was just a reporter, and that I should not colour the performance with any actor's characterization.

It was after this meeting that I began to realize the importance of the repetitions of, 'He said unto them', and, 'He answered and said unto them', and 'Jesus answering saith unto them'. These little phrases kept me in the role of the reporter. Without them I would be tempted to indulge in acting tricks, to forget that I was just a storyteller. These little phrases are the rocks on which the Gospel is built. What 'he said unto them' is what the Gospel is about.

When the donkey work of learning the lines was nearly done, I started to run the Gospel, recording the performances on a small portable tape-recorder. Often, during the run, the phone would ring and the recording would be broken off with an unsuitable expletive. Afterwards, I would play back the recording, and give myself notes. These notes filled many sheets of paper. They were not only corrections of any mistakes in the text, but also observations of interpretation. 'Introduce new character!' 'Don't gabble!' 'Plant this key word!' 'Increase the speed!' 'Don't get pious!', etc., etc.

Gradually an unexpected pattern emerged.

Whenever I did a serious and concentrated run-through of the Gospel, the performance seemed boring and lifeless. It would be correct, but uninteresting. But whenever I did a run-through, just for the fun of it, the performance was joyful and pleasing. This was very confusing for my puritanical nature. I thought that it must be a mistake. I tried to ignore it.

As an actor I have learnt to connect enjoyment with indulgence. Early on in my career, like most actors, I acted for the fun of it. I loved showing off. I was amazed at my cleverness. But, gradually, I discovered that the more I was enjoying myself when giving a performance, the less the audience seemed to enjoy it.

The best acting occurs when an actor totally dedicates himself to his performance – which means that he must forget himself and concentrate only on the character he is playing. And so one finds oneself in this awful trap. The initial lure of being an actor is the escape from real life, the fun of pretending to be someone else, the permitted make-believe. Then comes the depressing discovery that the enjoyment mustn't show. People should not come backstage and say: 'Well! *You* seemed to be enjoying yourself!' – as often happened to me when I was a young actor. *They* should be the ones enjoying themselves. They should not be aware of the actor's enjoyment. The actor's pride in his own tears. The actor's love of his own voice. The actor's joy in his gift of repartee. All this should be hidden . . .

And so we reach this sad conclusion: 'Bad acting is often enjoyable. Good acting is not.'

Damned shame!

As I have already written in the first part of this book, it was early in the London run of *Hadrian VII* that I discovered that I had lost some of my original seriousness in performance. This led to more laughs from the audience, but less real enjoyment, and less applause at the end. I had gradually forgotten the important element of Hadrian's *faith* – in my own pleasure at his colourful personality. The more I revelled in being Hadrian, the less effective I was in performance.

But now, with St Mark, I was becoming more and more aware that I *must* enjoy myself or the recital was lifeless. The old rules did not apply. I was no longer an actor, but a storyteller. A storyteller should enjoy himself. A good storyteller's enjoyment is infectious.

When I had finally finished learning my lines, I went down to Sandgate for a few days. I started to run the whole Gospel without a break; I needed to get used to the energy and concentration required. On the last day, when I was satisfied that I had reached performance level, I recorded the whole Gospel. Then I played it back.

It was terrible.

I found it impossible to listen to myself.

It was formal, lifeless, boring, monotonous . . .

I sat in silence . . . for a very long time.

I persuaded myself that studying the Gospel had been a rewarding experience for me. It had absorbed me for sixteen months. It had been a successful hobby.

But now, it seemed as if the hobby was over. I could not bring the Gospel to energetic life. I could not expect people to listen to it. It seemed as if I was defeated. I had forgotten that gospel means good news.

My father used to advise me that whenever I was at a low ebb, I should treat myself to a really good meal. He said that whenever I was down and out in spirits or in cash, I should feast myself.

That night in Sandgate I feasted.

At midnight I was feeling no pain; and, just for the fun of it, I started to recite St Mark. I switched on the tape-recorder. My performance seemed almost blasphemous with reckless enjoyment. I expected to be struck down. But for the first time, I really told the 'good news'. I told the 'good news' with confidence and love.

On 22 November 1977, alone at Sandgate, I gave a recital of St Mark's Gospel into a tiny tape-recorder.

Exactly a year later, on 22 November 1978, I gave the same recital at the White House.

*

I thought a great deal about where I should first perform St Mark. It would be a good idea to try it out as far away from London as possible.

The last week of the tour of *Antony and Cleopatra* was at the Theatre Royal, Newcastle, and one morning, after breakfast at the Turk's Head Hotel, I walked up the street to the newly built University Theatre.

I knew that the University Theatre had already fallen on hard times. It was going to be closed, but after a 'sit-in' by a group of actors, it had been taken over by British Actor's Equity.

When I arrived, at about 10.30, it seemed to be locked up. I knocked on the glass doors. Inside, a young lady was passing by. She opened the doors and asked me what I wanted. I told her my name, and asked to see the auditorium. She took me into the theatre, and I stood on the stage. I had once seen a friend in a show there. It had the right shape and feel to it.

The young lady was working on publicity for the theatre. I asked her who was in charge. She took me to the office of Keith Statham. He had not yet arrived, but I met his assistant, a lady who greeted me warmly. I asked whether they were having difficulty getting dates for the theatre. She told me that they had just been let down by a company who were due to visit the theatre the week of 12 December.

This was the week immediately after *Antony and Cleopatra* finished its final month's season at the Old Vic. It was the first time I would be free.

I offered my services. I asked whether they would be interested in my coming to the theatre to do a One Man Show. The lady thought that they would be interested. I offered to do the One Man Show for nothing. The lady thought that they would be even more interested.

She asked me the name of my One Man Show – and suddenly I was struck with panic. I stammered that I had not yet given it a title. She asked me what it was about. And I said, feebly, that it was a sort of recital from the Bible. Her enthusiasm seemed to diminish, but she said that she would talk to the director, Keith Statham, when he came in, and she advised me to telephone him.

I telephoned Keith Statham from London that weekend, and finally mustered up the courage to tell him the name of my One Man Show.

There was a pause and then he said. 'You *read* St Mark's Gospel?'

I said: 'No. I've learnt it.'

He said: 'Do you need any scenery?'

I said: 'Only a kitchen table and three chairs.'

He said: 'Is there a complicated lighting plot?'

I said: 'No. Turn them all on and leave them.'

He said: 'Do you wear black robes?'

I said: 'No. A light sports jacket.'

After careful consideration, Keith decided that I might do two performances, on 13 and 14 December. He said he would start the publicity. I asked him not to publicize it outside Newcastle.

The previous weekend I had received a surprising letter from Peter Gill, the director of Riverside Studios at Hammersmith.

I had visited the Riverside Studios early in the year when I was about halfway through learning St Mark. I saw a play written and directed by Peter Gill called *Small Change*. It was one of those rare magical evenings in the theatre when everything seemed to be absolutely right. The play was superbly written, acted and directed. But, in addition to these pleasures, the moment I walked into the theatre I knew that it would be the ideal place to do *St Mark*. It stayed in my mind throughout the year, and towards the end of the tour of *Antony and Cleopatra*, I was determined to get in touch with Peter Gill. It was in fact the very weekend when I planned to contact him that I received his letter. Peter wrote to ask if I would like to take part in a production he was to direct at the Riverside Studios in the New Year.

I telephoned him immediately, and told him that I was sorry that I didn't want to be in his production, but asked if we could meet. We fixed an appointment.

I vividly remember sitting by the river at Hammersmith – I had arrived much too early – and wondering about the step I was about to take. Also, although I had always admired his work, I hardly knew Peter Gill, and I had no idea what his reaction would be to my request.

It was a very calm reaction. He thought it sounded an interesting idea. He showed me round the studios. Building and decorating were going on. He talked of many plans and projects. He promised to let me know about *St Mark* as soon as possible. When I left him I knew that I had taken the right step, and felt strangely confident.

Within a week I was invited to do *St Mark's Gospel* at the Riverside Studios on four consecutive Sundays in the New Year.

Now I suddenly had two bookings.

But I was very aware of the fact that nobody had ever seen me do the performance.

It would be folly to expose myself to an audience without confirmation that I was not making a complete fool of myself.

Before going to Newcastle I arranged a Sunday afternoon run-through of *St Mark's Gospel* at the Riverside Studios, and invited Ronald Eyre, Peter Gill and Larry Dalzell to attend and give me their frank advice.

It was probably the most frightening occasion of my professional life. The day before the run-through I was so tense that I spent the afternoon in a sauna bath and nearly melted myself away.

Then, on the Sunday afternoon, as I left my flat and walked towards my car, a tiny little girl trotted towards me – she had obviously only just learnt to walk – and although I had never seen her before in my life, she looked up into my face and smiled with such affection and happiness, that all my fears vanished. They seemed ridiculous. It was the greatest smile that I have ever had.

It launched *St Mark*.

I collected Ronald and Larry and drove them to Hammersmith. Peter Gill was unable to join us, but his associates, David Gothard and John Burges, asked if they might take his place.

Riverside Studios were originally built for films and television and, as there were structural alterations being done in the main theatre, we used the dubbing room for the run-through. It was bitterly cold. I arranged my table and three chairs, and my audience of four sat huddled round a tiny electric fire.

I did the run-through.

Immediately afterwards, a discussion started.

It was *not* about me!

They talked about St Mark's Gospel.

The four of them talked enthusiastically about the emphasis on the miracles; the meaning of the parables; comparisons with other Gospels; the historical accuracy of the writing.

I stood and listened.

I supposed it had worked. They were obviously very stimulated by it.

And it certainly seemed as if my performance had not intruded!

Afterwards, I had dinner with Ron and Larry, and they gave me confirmation that it worked. Ron made some very helpful observations about the interpretation. He also gave me a wonderful piece of advice to remember before a performance.

He said, 'First approve of yourself. Then extend your approval to include other people.'

I wrote this down on the back of one of my lucky postcards of Key West, and took it with me to the University Theatre, Newcastle.

*

Most people are very nice to us, even if they have never been to a theatre in their lives, and have never heard of our names or of anything that we have done. 'Oh!' they say – rather as if they'd met someone wearing a funny paper hat – 'Oh! . . . that must be very interesting! Do you . . .?' And then their courage fails them; for they want to ask: 'Do you do it *all the time*? And do you actually *earn a living at it?*' But this is a rude thing to say to a stranger – even to a stranger who is closely related to a clown. Because most people have been to the circus and seen the clowns, and clowns not only wear funny hats, they paint their noses red, and put their feet into buckets of water, and fall on their backsides, and act in a gloriously undignified manner. So instead of asking: 'Do you do it all the time?' and: 'Do you actually earn a living at it?', they say: 'What are you doing at the moment?' – perhaps in the hope that you may get up and sing a song, or tell a joke, or do a dance – and the cares of this world would vanish, and they would be kids back at the circus again.

On the train to Newcastle I went to have lunch in the restaurant car, and was joined at the table by a young man who obviously wanted to talk. He asked me if I was going to Scotland, and if I thought the train was running on time, and if I did the journey often. And I replied rather grudgingly, and kept returning to my little paperback copy of St Mark's Gospel – taking good care not to let him see the title.

Finally, when lunch arrived, I started to make conversation, and discovered that his name was Trevor and that he lived in Blyth – and seemed dreadfully ashamed of it. Also, that he had just been 'down to London for one night, and stayed with a friend, and had a very good time', except that 'it had all been such a rush'. And I wondered *what* had all been such a rush, and wanted to ask him very personal questions. Instead, I asked him what he did for a living. And he said he worked in an office. And he asked me what I did for a living. And I said I was an actor.

'Oh . . .' he said. And he stared at me, looking for the paper hat. 'Oh . . . that must be very interesting! Do you . . .?' But his courage failed him, and, instead, he asked me: 'What are you doing at the moment?' And I said I was going to Newcastle to do a One Man Show.

This seemed to confuse him . . . I don't think he knew what I meant. He just continued to stare at me, as if I might suddenly get up and do a tap dance in the aisle, or turn the British Rail meal into Christmas dinner, or get down on my knees and sing 'Swannee'.

'Would I have seen you in anything?' he asked.

This is a hard one for the actor to answer. When you discover that your questioner has never been to the theatre, you have to start giving your television and movie credits.

'Did you see the Hitchcock film *Frenzy*?' I asked. He didn't think so – but he had heard of the title.

'Did you see *Travels with my Aunt*?' No, he didn't see it, and he had obviously never even heard of it.

'Did you see a television play recently about a man who lost his wife and got drunk in the cemetery sitting on her grave?'

'No . . .'

He looked at me as if I was making these things up. Then he asked me whether I had ever been in *Z Cars* or *Coronation Street* or *Crossroads* and I had to confess that I hadn't, and his interest in me waned and he looked out of the window. There would obviously be no cabaret with the biscuits and cheese. Still, I was the first actor he had met, and he would certainly tell his family in Blyth that he had had lunch on the train with, 'What was the name again?'

I felt as though I had let him down, and started to boast that I had worked with Diana Rigg and Penelope Keith, and he seemed to know those names and stared at me once more with wonder.

Then he asked me the name of my show in Newcastle.

'It's a recital,' I said, 'It's . . . it's something I've been working on. It's . . .' A long pause. 'I speak – some of the Bible – from memory.'

'From memory?' he said.

'Yes.'

'That must be difficult. How long did it take you to learn it?'

'Sixteen months,' I said.

He stared at me in disbelief. The waiter presented our bills and we paid them.

'Actually it's St Mark's Gospel. I do the whole of St Mark's Gospel from memory.'

He was a very nice, polite young man. He was not going to get a tap dance, or a conjuring trick, or a good joke. I was not in any television programme that he watched. I was obviously some sort of crank – even in my own bizarre profession.

'Well!' he said. 'That must be . . . That must be . . . very nice . . . Well!' He seemed relieved that we were parting, and shook my hand firmly.

'All the best!' he said.

'Thank you, Trevor,' I said. 'Try not to mind Blyth too much!'

'Give my regards to Diana Rigg,' he said – and left.

I pocketed my little paperback copy of St Mark's Gospel, and went back to my compartment.

At Newcastle I was met by Keith Statham. He seemed very subdued, and told me that the bookings for my two performances were not good.

We drove to a new hotel – which some fool had recommended. After checking in, I went up to my room, dumped my case on the bed, and noticed that the window looked rather askew. I went to investigate, and a huge pane of double-glazing started to fall out on top of my head. I managed to catch it, and staggered round the room beneath its weight. It didn't break, and I wasn't hurt, but I was very badly shaken. Immediately I went down to reception, told the tale, and demanded another room. This turned out to have a bathroom without light bulbs and a toilet that wouldn't flush. But there was no time for further complaints because a reporter with a tape-recorder had arrived. He sat on my bed, and I gave my first *St Mark* interview.

Then Keith whisked me off to the Tyne Tees Television Studios where, in thirty minutes, I was due to appear live on their local news programme.

This episode became a total nightmare.

We were ushered into a waiting-room and watched the news on a monitor. Then a young stage manager came in and started to give me instructions.

He said: 'First you'll do a ten-second teaser. Then there will be another item on film. Then you'll do a thirty-second teaser. And there'll be another item on film. Then you'll do a minute's teaser followed by the interview.'

I said: 'What do you mean by "teaser"?'

He said: 'Well, you know . . . your show.'

I said: 'You mean an excerpt?'

He said: 'Yes.'

I said: 'No!'

He said: 'You must! It's been planned.'

I said: 'I won't do any excerpts.'

He said: 'The producer has planned it.'

I said: 'Get the producer!'

He said: 'He's busy right now.'

I said: 'Get him!'

He left the room, and returned almost immediately to say that the producer couldn't be interrupted and that my first teaser was on in ten minutes. He then proceeded to tell me how the interview was going to be conducted.

He said: 'The interviewer will try to catch you out. For instance he might say, "Chapter 11, verse 9?" – and you'll answer whatever it is. And then he'll say, "Chapter 15, verse 31?" – and you'll answer whatever it is, and he'll carry on until he catches you out.'

I said: 'No!' very loudly, and started to tremble.

He said: 'I'm only telling you what I've been told.'

I said: 'Get the producer!' – and the clock ticked on.

Keith Statham sat there quietly watching the news.

A make-up girl arrived and dragged me off to have my face powdered and my hair combed, and started to talk about the weather.

The producer burst into the room and said: 'I understand you don't want to do the teasers?'

I said: 'No. Please, no! I'm not prepared to do that.'

He said: 'But we've planned it! The programme is arranged that way!'

I said: 'You'll have to change it!'

He said: 'There isn't time!'

I said: 'I don't care! I won't do it!'

He said: 'Will you please do just the one minute teaser? – Please! I beg you! And we'll cut out the others.'

I hesitated, and then said: 'All right. I'll do the Blind Bartimaeus story – but nothing else.'

He said: 'Fine!'

We were called on to the set, where two chairs were set for the interview, and I told the producer it was no use the interviewer trying to catch me out with chapter and verse questions, because I wouldn't be able to answer them. He looked glum, and said that unfortunately the interviewer was not their regular Arts and Entertainments man but another correspondent, who knew nothing about the theatre or religion.

I was introduced to this correspondent. He looked ghastly white. The producer left us.

157

Suddenly I became very calm, and told the interviewer not to worry. I assured him that he would not need to ask me the trick questions.

Then, as other items in the programme were going out in other parts of the studio, we whispered together.

He said that he'd been told that I was trying to break the record of someone who'd learnt the *Koran*, and thought to conduct the interview on the lines of 'Mr Amazing Memory Man'.

I said that I didn't know that anyone had ever learnt the *Koran*, and that I wasn't trying to break any memory records.

I suggested that he asked me why I chose St Mark, and leave the rest to me.

We were cued by the floor manager.

I took a deep breath, remembered the lines, 'Take no thought beforehand what ye shall speak, neither do ye premeditate', and did the six verses about Blind Bartimaeus.

The interview proceeded smoothly, with the minimum of questions. The only sign of tension was towards the end when I told a story about my father and used the words, 'And he said unto me' – quite unconsciously . . . and the camera crew laughed, and the interviewer laughed, and I laughed, and everything ended happily.

Then we all went and had a drink; and the producer and Keith and I exchanged music-hall stories – and I wondered, with an actor's vanity, whether Trevor had been watching.

Later that evening, Keith took me to his home and became distinctly less subdued. He revealed himself to be a composer and a marvellous pianist. And his wife, Ruth, was one of those rare people with whom I felt an instant friendship. We had an Italian meal together, and I returned to the dreadful hotel feeling relaxed and happy.

It didn't last.

There was a large party of drunken Norwegian tourists on my floor, who shouted, broke glasses, and sang carols, and no amount of protesting from the rest of us could stop them. Finally, at about four in the morning, the police were brought in and they were silenced. I slept fitfully, dreaming of a public biblical interrogation, while holding up an enormous pane of glass over my head.

In the morning I went to the theatre and met my volunteer

stage-manager and electrician. We found a suitable table and three chairs, and did the lighting.

Then I went to have lunch by myself at the Turk's Head – where, of course, I should have been staying. In the afternoon I looked at my words, and had a little sleep.

I have no recollection of going to the theatre, but a tremendous calm came over me just before the performance, and before walking on stage I murmured to the stage-manager, 'God bless!'

I took on my little tape-recorder, and recorded the whole recital for future reference. I told the audience it was so that I could check my mistakes in the morning. They didn't laugh. They didn't make a sound for the entire two-hour recital; except that after the interval during the verses about the transfiguration, some students in the front rows made a deafening noise finishing off packets of potato crisps.

I got through the whole thing without making any serious mistakes, and the little audience clapped warmly as I walked off-stage.

I went to my dressing-room, lit a cigarette, and sat down.

Several minutes went by. Nobody came to see me.

Sixteen months' work was over.

Sixteen months, waking at dawn, studying St Mark verse by verse.

Suddenly the door crashed open, and a large, dishevelled young man staggered into the room. He said: 'I'm a painter. I want to ask you one question.' I said: 'What is it?' He said: 'Why the hell did you learn it? Why didn't you just read it?' I suppressed a rising desire to sob, and heard myself shouting at him: 'Why don't you just take photographs?' He stared at me, smiled and said: 'Point taken. I'll buy you a pint!'

Then Keith looked in and said that he had been unable to attend the performance because of work, but that a Regional Equity official who called to discuss business, had sneaked in at the beginning, and found it quite difficult to tear himself away . . .

Then I had to meet members of the theatre club – mostly elderly people – who said it had been 'as good as a play', and that they'd 'listened to every word', and 'Whatever made you do it?'

After a wildly indigestible Chinese meal, I went back to the hotel. Massed bands might have been playing in the next room; Concorde might have been circling over head; but I slept peacefully.

The next day I awoke thinking of the painter's question: 'Why did you learn it?'

Need I have learnt it?

Should I have learnt it?

Was the whole performance an act of indulgence?

Was I trying to set myself up as a close relative of the Almighty?

Was it an act of disgusting exhibitionism? If people wanted to read St Mark, they could easily do so without any help from me.

I walked to the theatre to see if 'word of mouth' had encouraged any more bookings for the second performance. It hadn't.

There was no review in the paper.

Above all, I suddenly realized that I wanted a reaction from a member of the clergy. Keith told me that he had sent invitations to all the churches in the city, but not a single member of the clergy had found time to come. 'It's very near Christmas, and we're very busy . . .'

It really felt like a non-event.

Remembering my father's advice, I went to a splendid restaurant called Moores, and had a very good meal. It helped.

Before the performance that evening, I was told that the theatre chaplain would like to meet me. Having been trapped in dressing-rooms with theatre chaplains, I agreed to meet him in the front-of-house bar. He was an attractive young man called Fr Peter Strange. He was a little shy, but obviously very knowledgeable and enthusiastic about the theatre, and we talked together easily. I found myself telling him the story of the painter, and how the question, 'Why did you learn it?' had filled me with doubts. Fr Peter did not comment, but I gathered that he was coming to the performance, and I hoped for some reaction from him afterwards.

It seemed to be much livelier the second time, and I started to relax with the words; but towards the end of the recital I felt extremely tired, and even wondered whether I would be able to finish it.

Afterwards, Fr Peter greeted me in the bar. He said,

160

immediately, 'Of course you had to learn it! Learning it makes it an act of faith! Learning it makes all the difference!'

I do not know whether he realized how much his words meant to me.

They were some of the most welcome words I have ever heard.

I wanted to hug him; but he went on to talk of details, and how he had forgotten the verse, 'And there were also with him other little ships,' in the storm scene, and how amusingly I pronounced the word Boanerges (meaning I had got it wrong), and the moment of gratitude passed – until I wrote to him months later to express my thanks.

Keith and Ruth had also seen the performance, and seemed to have been stimulated by it. I took them to supper, and Ruth asked many questions and made many comments, and told me how amusingly I pronounced the word Sadducees (meaning I had got it wrong).

We parted outside the hotel. Newcastle suddenly looked very beautiful, and even the hotel seemed friendly.

*

It felt like a return from the moon when I got home. This was not because of Newcastle, but because for such a long time I had been so totally absorbed in St Mark and had not had another important thought in my head. I must have been very poor company.

On the evening of my return to London I went to have a drink with a visiting friend from America at the Savoy. I mentioned, casually, that I had just done a recital of St Mark's Gospel. But he said, sharply, 'I don't wish to know about that!'

Another friend had reacted in the same way. He had said, 'What on earth do you want to do *that* for!' – as if I had been beating up old ladies.

Puzzling.

But other people were more encouraging. On the Friday of that week, I took part in a poetry and music recital in aid of St Martin's in the Fields, with Peter Gale, Julia McKenzie, Michael Williams and Judi Dench. The comparative lack of responsibility must have gone to my head, and I performed with the confidence of Max Bygraves. Judi Dench is an old friend, and for years I have teased her about her poetry recitals.

As well as her theatre work, Judi has always found time to give innumerable poetry recitals up and down the country, and I have always pretended to be very jealous. In the pub – after our performance – I told her, smugly, about *St Mark* – thinking to up-stage her. But she disarmed me immediately by her enthusiasm for the idea.

Among the chief delights of being an actor is that it is quite impossible to predict what one may find oneself doing next. My engagements for 1977 finished unexpectedly with a visit to Pebble Mill Studios, Birmingham, to read *The African Queen* for BBC radio. This was in five half-hour episodes. The memory of the film proved too much for me. I was not good as Humphrey Bogart – but my Katharine Hepburn was a credit.

During the three weeks before my first Sunday performance at Riverside, I did not think much about *St Mark*. Like most actors, I have a defence mechanism which guards me against disappointments, lessens expectations, and deadens the possibility of defeat. It did not seem likely, on the evidence of Newcastle, that my recital of St Mark would cause much of a stir, and I did not want to hurt myself by expecting success, and receiving only faint praise or even indifference.

Of course, this is a game that actors play. My expectations were in fact very high. It seemed to me that *St Mark should* succeed. My faith in the idea of the recital was colossal. But my faith in my own ability to succeed was not as great. There is a gap between the performance one thinks one is giving and the performance the audience actually sees – and it is always a shock to discover this discrepancy. It is an affront to one's conceit. The actor must believe in himself – or he will never muster up the courage to walk on-stage. The actor must believe that he is a genius, a unique revelation of humanity. But the actor must expect that the audience will not see it in quite the same way. The actor must expect that there may be some error in communication – over which he has no final control . . .

Because of the extensive re-structuring and decorating, it seemed unlikely that Riverside Studios would be ready for my opening performance on Sunday, 8 January. Builders, plumbers and electricians were everywhere. Planks of wood, coils of wire, buckets of paint, and debris filled the building.

Amidst this chaos, Peter Gill smiled calmly and continued to rehearse his actors in *The Cherry Orchard* which was to open on the previous evening, Saturday the 7th. When I called in on the Friday afternoon, he saw my consternation at the state of the building and invited me to watch his cast practising a dance. It was strangely therapeutic.

Then, on Friday evening, I went with my friend Patience Collier to see John Gielgud at the Cottesloe Theatre in a new play called *Half Life*. In the first act, Sir John had a little hesitation with his lines, but his performance was so alive and energetic that it really did not matter. And in the second act he was absolutely superb. Although in his seventies, Sir John makes many young actors look old fashioned and inept. We called backstage to see him and he apologized for his lapses in Act I. He said he was a little tired as he had been recording that day at the BBC for five solid hours and, in any case, because of the repertory system, he hadn't done *Half Life* for three weeks. I felt ashamed of my nervousness about *St Mark*, and looked with enormous affection at this wonderful actor. His achievements are so great, and his personality has remained so unaffected.

It seems as if the really great actors retain the nervousness and enthusiasm of children. I remember colliding with Laurence Olivier backstage at the Old Vic when I was playing with the National. I was in the middle of a matinée of *Equus*, and he was rehearsing upstairs in the dusty rehearsal room with Franco Zeffirelli for the play *Saturday, Sunday, Monday*. He grabbed hold of me and said: 'What do you do when a director gives you business before you've learnt your lines? Franco keeps giving me business and I can't do it because I don't know my lines yet!' There was a call over the speaker, and he cried desperately, 'Oh God, they're calling me! I don't know what I'm going to do!'

At the time I was greatly heartened by Sir Laurence's nervousness. It is good to know one's peers are human . . . And the marvellous performance of Sir John in *Half Life* – after he had done a day's recording and after he had had three weeks away from the play – inspired me before doing *St Mark*.

By now, my lucky postcard of Key West was covered with helpful instructions and warnings. I culled old adages like a greedy antique collector.

Perhaps the most difficult part of any performance is to start it. The temptation is to give the entire performance with the first line. There is a compulsion to manufacture magic like a magician or a hypnotist; to dazzle the audience into instant submission. This is ridiculous vanity. I wrote down: 'Any starting point is flawed.' I warned myself: 'Accept approximation!' I tried to remember that: 'Fragmentation makes the whole.'

There is a silly habit of thinking of an audience as an enemy. I wrote: 'The audience has made a sincere act of hope.' I even made a little list of favourite people and imagined I was playing solely for them.

I tried to convince myself that: 'A man is most alive when his security is taken away from him.' And this was the most helpful piece of advice of all.

Before doing a play you may be struck with terror – but at least you are about to pretend to be someone else. You are dressed in someone else's clothes; you have probably altered your appearance with make-up and a wig; and you are working with equally vulnerable and frightened colleagues.

Before doing my One Man Show, with no disguise, and no characterization, and no colleagues, I felt totally exposed and naked.

But then I would be challenged by the actual material. Then, the mystery of the Gospel itself would take over. Then, the implications of this story would make me realize my insignificance. Finally, the words of Christ echo in the mind: 'Why are ye so fearful? how is it that ye have no faith?'

Invariably before doing *St Mark*, I have been possessed with a great calm and feelings of intense joy.

Although they didn't tell me beforehand, I have since discovered that there were only four bookings for my performance at Riverside Studios on that first Sunday matinée. However, about a hundred and fifty people turned up at the doors. Geoffrey Burridge had loyally recruited a group of unsuspecting acquaintances to fill up seats, and my dear friends, Pinkie Johnstone, Ellen Pollock and Anna Massey, were there. The reception of the recital was warm and friendly, and after the performance people said nice things. A small party of us went and had hamburgers with a lot of tomato sauce.

Among the audience were the critics Michael Billington and Bernard Levin. The next day Michael Billington wrote in the *Guardian*: 'Down in the smoky suburb of Hammersmith, the

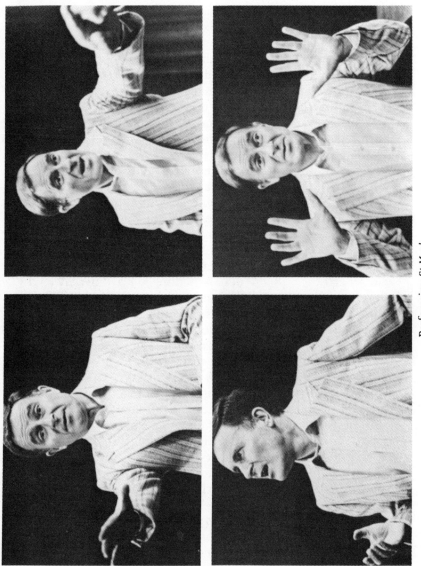

Performing St. Mark

Riverside Studios offered a rare treat: Alec McCowen narrating St Mark's Gospel. Sporting a red open-necked shirt, fawn trousers and suede shoes and patrolling the vast spaces of a pinewood stage, McCowen related the familiar story with all the precision, irony, intelligence and faintly controlled anger that characterizes all his work. It was not only a remarkable feat of memory: it was also a superb piece of acting.' He also wrote: 'Agnostics, atheists and believers can, in fact, all get pleasure out of this remarkable performance (to be repeated over the next three Sundays). Free from the reverend boom that often overtakes actors when they get a Bible in their hands, it handled the language of the King James Version with surgical care, abundant wit and springy intelligence.'

As a result of this review, the bookings at Riverside increased considerably. On the following Sunday, Bernard Levin wrote in the *Sunday Times* of 'the power and glory of the two hours in which this usually cool and classical actor transcends his own style, extends his very considerable talents, and speaks language that has no peer anywhere in our literature other than the works of Shakespeare. And then, as we listen, the whole (language and actor together) is fused into something on a different level entirely by the overwhelming and urgent life of the story; it is simply not to be missed by anyone with ears, a mind or a soul, let alone all three'.

After this, all the performances were sold out in advance, and I agreed to do an extra two matinées.

Each Sunday at Riverside was like a colossal party. After the recital, friends, family, colleagues and strangers would come backstage or congregate at the bar and talk about *St Mark*.

Requests to do the recital started to come in from all over the country, from theatres, churches and schools.

The BBC wanted to broadcast it.

The producer, Arthur Cantor, wanted to present me in America, and almost immediately offered a week at Harvard in the autumn.

By chance, Katharine Hepburn read about it in Hollywood, and advised her friend Alan Shayne, the President of Warner Brothers Television, to make a bid to televise the recital. He sent representatives and beat the English television companies with their offers.

Two London managements wanted to present me for seasons

166

in West End theatres. However, I was not yet sure that I could perform *St Mark* on a regular theatre schedule – involving eight performances a week – and I turned these offers down.

As happened after *Hadrian VII* opened in London, I was interviewed, photographed and fêted. After the depression of the previous year, everything seemed to be coming up roses . . . The kaleidoscope had changed again.

Ironically, Larry Dalzell, knowing that I was in a parlous financial state, had fixed up two movies and a television play to be done in February and March, which meant that I wouldn't be free to do *St Mark* again until April.

As Riverside Studios had a full programme lined up for several months, I wondered where the next best place would be.

And naturally I thought of the Mermaid.

I wrote to Sir Bernard Miles asking whether he would be interested in presenting me – preferably at weekends or in repertory. Typically, he was on the phone at nine o'clock the next day, full of enthusiasm for the idea, and chiding me for not coming to him first. He threatened to empty St Paul's Cathedral, and fill the Mermaid with the devout. He envisaged brass bands playing hymns, and massed choirs crying hallelujah! We made a provisional date in April for me to give three performances a week for a two-month season.

Meanwhile I had a small part in the movie *Stevie*, playing a comical love scene with the super-professional Glenda Jackson. Also, because he was in the film, I met one of my favourite actors, Trevor Howard, and told him that years ago he had strongly influenced my career.

A film company had offered me a seven-year film contract. I had to go to their offices in Soho Square to complete the deal. While I was sitting in their waiting-room, I picked up a movie magazine and my eyes immediately fell on a quotation from Trevor Howard. 'Any young actor who signs a long contract with a British film company is doomed . . . Doomed I tell you!' I fled.

At last I was able to thank Mr Howard, and also to tell him that for years I had hoped that he would make a movie with Spencer Tracy and Jean Gabin. The combination of these three extraordinarily sensitive and rugged men would have been irresistible.

With Glenda Jackson in *Stevie*

After *Stevie*, rehearsals started for a television play called *When the Actors Come*, written and directed by Don Taylor.

It is best to avoid television in January, February or March if you have any fears for your health. Unless you are fortunate enough to be working in one of the company rehearsal rooms, you are invariably deposited in a freezing, draughty Territorial Hall, a disused school, or a condemned morgue. Texts, and fading photographs of Princess Alice, Countess of Athlone, the Princess Royal or Lord Baden-Powell decorate the peeling walls; and acoustics are so bad that it is impossible to hear a cue. Actors huddle together with cracked cups of instant coffee, and mutter miserably that they have been called to rehearsal much too early, and make gloomy counter-revolutionary noises about the preoccupation of Equity with the Rule Book instead of actual conditions of work. The only thing worse than these conditions is to be involved in winter television filming. On location one has no dressing-room, and not even a chair of one's own during the waits between shots, and actors often have to beg kindly wardrobe or make-up crews to allow them to use the wardrobe or make-up vans for a bit of shelter.

When the Actors Come was about the Peasants' Revolt in Hungary. After a week of rehearsing in a barn set in the middle of a sea of mud in darkest Chiswick – where the overseer kept forgetting to turn on the heating – there was a small actors' revolt, and rehearsals were transferred to the old Lime Grove Television Studios at Shepherds Bush. Here, the wind rattled through the building, and the cold was just as intense, but at least we could sometimes slip away and warm up with a quick glass of rum in the bar.

When I was a young actor I had done many *live* television plays from Lime Grove. I remembered the excitement of phoning home from the studio call-box at the bottom of the iron stairs, after the transmission, to get the family's reaction. 'Could you see me, Mother?' 'Was Dad pleased?' 'Was it a good picture?' 'Did you notice my dresser hand me my hat?' 'Did you see the scenery wobble when I opened the door the wrong way?' 'Did you hear the crash when they dropped the plate?', etc., etc.

It was an exhilarating time. By today's standards productions were often rough and ready but, by God, they were alive! The sound boom was frequently in picture, quick changes were sometimes incomplete, actors took prompts when they forgot lines, and complicated sets were crammed into a tiny area. During a live transmission, a stage-manager would take the bemused actor's hand as he left one set, and lead him like a child through a hurdle course of scenery to a set on the other side of the studio – while, on the way, dressers would hurriedly brush clothes, and make-up girls would hurriedly powder faces, and the whispered instruction might be given to hurry it up or slow it down, and the warning might be given that a door had stuck or a prop had been lost or that a fellow actor had fainted.

It was good to be back at Lime Grove and remember the callow lovers I used to play, but difficult to realize that now a good-looking actress was actually calling me father!

It was a happy company. I particularly enjoyed an interlude when Michael Graham Cox played a studio piano, and Ursula Howells, Zena Walker, Rosemary McHale, Patrick Stewart and the whole frozen cast forgot the Hungarian Revolution and sang a defiant selection of musical comedy favourites, shaking the dust down from that old entertainment factory in Shepherds Bush.

My third job during this period was in a movie called *Hanover*

Street, in which my character – the head of something or other – was chiefly required to smoke a pipe. I had to send Christopher Plummer on a secret mission to get 'the papers' or destroy 'the papers', and tell the lovely Leslie Ann Down that her husband was missing, and in each scene I packed my pipe, and lit my pipe, and smoked my pipe, and complained about the flavour, and emptied my pipe, and then repeated the process with a different tobacco. And not being a pipe-smoker, by the end of the day my mouth and throat were raw with this unaccustomed behaviour. It was a relief to get back to the simpler exercise of reciting the whole of St Mark's Gospel.

During this period I had given single performances of *St Mark* at the Royal Exchange Theatre, Manchester, at the Playhouse, Nottingham, and the Maddermarket Theatre, Norwich – where I had once been a student of Nugent Monck and swept the stage for ten shillings a week.

Then, on 16 April, I opened *St Mark* at the Mermaid Theatre.

It was exactly ten years since the opening of *Hadrian VII*, and on Tuesday, 18 April, after my performance, Bernard Miles gave an anniversary party on the stage. There was a happy reunion with Peter Dews, Peter Luke, Maggie Courtenay, Donald Eccles, Brian Coburn and many of the old gang.

And happily, as with *Hadrian VII*, all the seats for my two month's season were soon sold. Bernard had sent out three thousand leaflets advertising *St Mark's Gospel* to London churches and to seventy magazines 'purporting to preach Christianity'. He wrote to me: 'We expect the buggers to turn up in large numbers.'

They did.

Soon they were sitting in the aisles; and Bernard decided to install closed circuit television in the theatre restaurant for the overflow audience. I was playing in repertory with the hit play *Whose Life is it Anyway?* and the Mermaid was bursting at its seams.

The Archbishop of Canterbury, Dr Coggan, and his wife, came backstage with a photographer who shouted at me: 'Put your arm round the Archbishop!' I looked very embarrassed – and Dr Coggan put his arm around *me*. We had a very interesting conversation about Mark – and, as he left, the Archbishop made the charming remark: 'I wish you could teach some of my boys how to speak!'

After the performance on another evening, I was quietly entertaining the Bishops of Kensington and Winchester and their wives, when two ebullient New York friends, Arnold Weisberger and Milton Goldman, burst into the dressing-room. Introductions were made, and there was a slight hiatus as these somewhat disparate people looked at each other. Then Milton decided to relax us all with a religious joke. 'A nun tells the Mother Superior, "We have a case of syphilis in the nunnery." And she says, "Oh good! I'm getting tired of the Beaujolais!"' . . . There was a slight pause. The Bishops and their wives looked stunned, Arnold and Milton roared with laughter . . . and I poured myself a stiff drink.

I was asked to take part in a dialogue with Joseph McCulloch at his church, St Mary le Bow, and he raised the question which seemed to trouble many of the clergy who came to *St Mark*. The last twelve verses are believed to have been added on to the Gospel at a much later period. Many people complain of a difference in style, and, evidently, the promises of Jesus that believers 'shall take up serpents; and if they drink any deadly thing it shall not hurt them' are mocked by sceptics. But, since these last twelve verses describe Jesus after his resurrection, they seem to me to be vital to the telling of the story. In our dialogue I flatly rejected Joseph McCulloch's objections to the lines, arrogantly proclaimed, '*I* like them!' and got an unexpected round of applause from the audience.

I purposely presented the last three chapters with simplicity and no trace of theatricality, so it was a surprise to get a letter from a clergyman who suggested that the lights should dim when I said, 'there was darkness over the whole land until the ninth hour' – and should brighten during the resurrection. I was even more surprised to get another letter suggesting that, as I was speaking the words of God, an electrician should devise a halo about my head.

During the Mermaid season I also gave single performances at Strode College in Somerset (awfully good fish and chips afterwards in Phillip Levitt's kitchen); at Broadcasting House, where it was recorded in the basement – to the loud accompaniment of the underground, and – surprisingly – in Denmark, for the Danish-British Society in Copenhagen. There was a catering strike in Copenhagen, and at the hotel my breakfast tray was unexpectedly loaded – by the obviously keen stand-by staff – with scrambled eggs for three, a large omelette, and a pint of milk. However, I was beautifully looked after by a lively little lady called Helen Hansen. She drove me to Elsinore; I saw the famous Little Mermaid, and was proud to hear that Vera Lynn was singing in the Tivoli Gardens.

As soon as the Mermaid season finished, I did two performances for the Greenwich Festival, and then, on 20 June, started a four-week season for the H. M. Tennent Management at the Comedy Theatre in the heart of the West End of London. It was a thrill to see *St Mark's Gospel* in neon lights outside the theatre, and an even greater thrill to see lines of people at the box-office waiting for returned seats.

I was now giving six performances a week, including a matinée on Sunday. This matinée was the cause of a lot of publicity when British Actor's Equity tried to ban it. At that time there was no agreement between Equity and West End managements with regard to Sunday performances, and the union did not wish to start a precedent. However, since an official at Equity had already agreed that *The Two Ronnies* could give four Sunday matinées of their revue at the London Palladium, there was naturally cause for ridicule. I was very sad that at no time did Equity contact me personally, and wrote a highly emotional letter to the Council. This was never acknowledged – but agreement was finally given that the Gospel could be spoken on the Sabbath, and this was always the most popular performance.

On my final Sunday there was a line of people hoping to get into the theatre which, I was told, could only be compared with the crowds trying to get into the newly opened hit musical *Evita*.

It was a very happy time – partly owing to the loving administration of Michael Ginesi, the General Manager of the Comedy Theatre – and the producers asked me to extend the season. Reluctantly, I had to refuse, because I was very tired and needed a rest before going to America.

My most vivid memory of performing *St Mark* is of that very private time before the performance, standing alone in the wings, waiting for the house lights to go down, hearing the noise of the people out front, and wondering whether it is really going to be possible to quieten them and compel them to listen. To the lone actor, a very large audience makes a frightening noise. It sounds like a thousand-tongued monster. It is easy to imagine hostility. It is easy to anticipate derision. One feels small, hesitant and feeble. Often there is a delay because of a double booking, or because of a party of latecomers. And then, suddenly, the stage-manager will wave a warning hand, the house lights will dim, and the noise will gradually diminish. In his mind the actor must transform this thousand-tongued monster into a small friendly family party, and the auditorium to a familiar sitting-room. The first activity must be to greet the people. The actor becomes host; and the guests must be put at ease.

During my recitals of St Mark I became quite adept at opening speeches of welcome, taking into account the place and time of the performance. At the Mermaid, I recalled my paternal grandfather, and this led to a tribute to Sir Bernard Miles. At the Comedy, I recalled a boyhood visit to that theatre to see a revue, and remembered sitting entranced at Judy Campbell singing 'A Nightingale Sang in Berkeley Square'. In New York I recalled a stage-door encounter with the great American solo performer, Ruth Draper. I hoped that these introductions would disarm audiences expecting a religious experience, and stop them from investing the occasion with any artificial reverence. Also, I hoped that by chatting in a casual manner, I would relax my voice and be able to launch into the Gospel in a natural conversational way.

There were two other reasons for these introductions. They gave latecomers an extra five minutes to get to their seats; and they enabled me to deal with any unexpected contingencies – on some occasions to ask for an increase or a decrease in the heating of the theatre; and on one occasion, at a college, to ask if the noise of disco music from an adjoining building could be lowered. There was certainly an advantage to being on my own. It is not possible for Antony to interrupt a speech to Cleopatra, 'Let Rome in Tiber melt, and the wide arch of the ranged empire fall! Here is my space – and would you mind turning down the heating?'

However, once I had started on the Gospel, it was not possible or advisable to interrupt it. Only once, in another college theatre, I actually left the stage to stop some hammering that was going on in an adjoining scene-shop. The hammering couldn't be heard by the audience, but I couldn't concentrate, and was beginning to make spoonerisms.

I suppose my biggest neurosis as an actor is noise – unnecessary noise, made by fellow workers in the theatre. Ushers talking, barmaids chatting, and – worst of all – fellow actors whispering in the wings. Before starting any new production I usually have sleepless nights anticipating noise. Distracting noise; sabotaging noise; damaging, insensitive, destructive bloody noise. Of course, I have frequently been reprimanded for the same thoughtless behaviour to my colleagues, but, in my egomania, this does not seem anything like as important . . .

Now that my American trip was imminent, I began to have nightmares about New York noise – remembering the stage crew's radio and television sets, remembering loud-voiced stage-doormen, remembering the electricians in *Hadrian VII* and the occasion when I left the stage in the middle of a quiet scene and invited them to entertain the audience – since they were making a good deal more noise than the actors.

However, before going to America, there was one more recital of St Mark in England. In 1968, as I have written, we gave a special matinée of *Hadrian VII* for the Lambeth Conference at the Mermaid. Now, in another amazing coincidence, I was invited to go to Canterbury to do *St Mark* for the 1978 Conference. The Conference was held at the University of Kent, and it was proposed that I should give the recital in Rutherford Hall – which has a magnificent view of Canterbury Cathedral through its centre window. Unfortunately the Hall has a dreadful acoustic. I called to make a preliminary inspection, and was assured that a Mr Geoffrey Yates, of Christian Audio Vision Services, would make me perfectly audible with a throat microphone.

He did.

I suppose if ever I should have been nervous with *St Mark* it was before reciting it in front of 400 bishops. But on a beautiful summer's evening, I drove from Sandgate, through the lovely leafy Kentish lanes, rich with honeysuckle and wild roses, to the ancient City of Canterbury, and found myself singing at the top of my voice 'To be a Pilgrim'.

It was a wonderfully happy performance and, obviously, from the reaction of the audience, perfectly audible. Afterwards I was entertained by a small party of English and American bishops and archbishops – and marvelled at the outcome of my early morning hobby. Finally, Dr Coggan shouted good-naturedly at his colleagues: 'Let this man go home and rest!' and I drove back to Sandgate.

After a few days by the sea, tramping the beach at Littlestone and Greatstone, I returned to London, spent a week in the comforting old womb of Broadcasting House doing the narration for a twelve-part serial of *Vanity Fair*, happily turned down a role in a forthcoming movie of *Dracula*, and flew to New York.

*

New York was wilder than ever.

My friendly producer, Arthur Cantor, characteristically full of enthusiasm and future plans, met me at the airport, and we drove into the hot and smoggy city. The Meurice was no longer a hotel, and I was booked into the Alrae on the East Side. Waiting for me in my room were the usual flowers and whisky. My agent, Robert Lantz, telephoned and I thanked him for the flowers. He said he'd sent the whisky. The doorbell rang, and a reporter from the *Christian Science Monitor* arrived. We had an hour's interview. He left, but, before I could finish unpacking, the doorbell rang again and I met my American stage-manager. His name was Larry Bussard. He looked about eleven years old, but I sensed a reassuring, tough efficiency under the smiling schoolboy face. We discussed the stage furniture and lighting, and fixed a time to meet the following day. The telephone rang, and Arthur Cantor's press-agent, George Willard, informed me that a lady from the *New Yorker Magazine* would interview me the following day at the theatre, and another lady reporter would meet me for tea. An official of Warner Brothers rang to ask if I could lunch with the director, Michael Lindsay Hogg. A television producer's secretary rang to arrange for me to appear on an early morning television Chat Show. She said she thought they'd want me to do an excerpt from 'your show'. I refused, which threw her into total confusion. She said she'd call me back. I decided not to finish unpacking, and fled from the hotel to have a quiet dinner with Gil Parker.

I was to do *St Mark's Gospel* for a three-week season at a splendid small theatre called The Marymount which is part of a Catholic College on East 71st Street.

After the second preview, I met Arthur Cantor's co-producer, the lovely film actress Greer Garson. She came into my dressing-room with tears in her eyes and, although she was wearing a tuxedo, there was no mistaking Mrs Miniver. We embraced immediately – like long-parted friends – and she told me she was deeply moved by the recital. She said, 'Why should the devil have all the best tunes?' We were joined by Arthur Cantor, who was obviously delighted that, despite the fact that the newspapers were on strike, the whole season was already sold out. Then he suggested that the three of us should meet the following morning to look at a bigger theatre for a return engagement.

The next day Arthur and I collected Greer at her hotel and she seemed somewhat distracted. Then, while rummaging in her large handbag, looking for some missing keys, she took out a tiny silver mouth organ and played two choruses of 'Old MacDonald had a Farm'. I was a little surprised at this, but Arthur didn't seem concerned, and it obviously made Greer feel much better.

It was the day of my official New York first night, and I was feeling very tense. After inspecting the theatre, Arthur suggested lunch and said, 'I know this great Greek restaurant!' But Greer, noticing my look of nausea, suddenly took over and insisted that we return to her hotel where she promised to look after me. She told me to keep quiet and let her do the talking. She talked of her early theatre days in England, and carefully chose my lunch. 'A small bowl of consommé, followed by a plain omelette.' She reconsidered this and then told the waiter: 'No! I think he can manage an omelette *fines herbes*!' When I had finished eating, she looked at me sympathetically and said: 'You don't want any coffee, do you?' I murmured tearfully, 'No.' And she said, 'Then off you go, straight to bed!' . . . I loved Greer Garson.

Strangely, *St Mark's Gospel* attracted many of the great ladies of the screen and theatre, and I delighted in visits backstage from Katharine Hepburn, Ingrid Bergman, Lauren Bacall, Lillian Gish, Helen Hayes, Louise Rainer and Ruth Gordon.

After the first night, Alan Shayne gave a party for me on behalf of Warner Brothers, and Greer, the red-haired queen of Texas, dazzled many of my movie-mad friends.

The reviews in *Newsweek* – 'Mark of Genius' – *Time Magazine*, and the *New Yorker*, were glowing, and Arthur's office was soon besieged with requests for me to do *St Mark* all over the country.

Backstage, after the performance, religious groups would get wildly mixed up with show-business personalities, and I particularly remember the evening when I was being given a Citation, and Carol Channing – complete with *both* her eyelashes – suddenly emerged from the middle of a Bible Society.

With Carol Channing

On another evening, I heard the mother of an actor friend come backstage during the interval halfway through the performance, and ask to see me. She was asked if she could possibly come back at the end, and she said in a very surprised voice: 'Oh! Is there more?'

Larry Bussard proved to be not only a marvellous stage-manager, but also a remarkably fearless bodyguard, protecting me from religious fanatics who sometimes lay in wait outside the theatre with biblical re-writes. He also had an unforgettable way of knocking at my door before the performance, smile and murmur apologetically, 'It's places!'

In England, when the stage-management call the actors to the stage, they say 'Beginners, please!'

In America they simply say, 'Places!'

Larry had a way of saying 'It's places!' which somehow implied that an exhausting sexual orgy was about to take place – and he doubted if I had the energy to go through with it.

Unfortunately he was unable to come on tour with me, but I was lucky to obtain the services of Keith Waggoner, another superb stage-manager and guardian. Keith is one of those people I never expect to find in the theatre. A quiet, bearded Kansan, he seemed to have strayed right off the farm – and he always carried with him a gentle and bemused air of surprise at the antics of us town folks. He has a marvellous sense of humour, and referred to my solo performance of *St Mark* in the words of *Variety* as 'A Class Act'. I don't think I could have endured the demands of the ensuing tours without his company.

When the three-week season at The Marymount was over, we drove to East Hartford for my first performances in an American college. I lived on the campus, and found that I was totally accepted by the students. They smiled and continually asked me: 'How ya doin'?'

Then I played a week at Harvard, and a week at the Cleveland Playhouse. I also managed to have a few days' driving in Vermont at the height of the fall.

We returned to New York for another three-week season, this time at the Playhouse Theatre, a converted church on West 48th Street in the district known as Hell's Kitchen.

At the end of the second New York engagement I was suffering from a congested chest, spasmodic deafness, and exhaustion.

An ear specialist had told me that the deafness was caused by the congested chest.

The exhaustion was mainly caused by the demands of *St Mark*, and by kindness.

The kindness of friends and acquaintances in New York.

The never-ending invitations to lunches, suppers, drinks, shows, a little 'get-together', a big 'get-together', – 'whatever'.

At my last performance – a Sunday matinée – it was a great effort to get through the recital. I was stifling coughs, trembling, and forcing my concentration.

Then there were the backstage visitors to greet, friends and strangers, and the usual questions to answer.

'How did you think of it in the first place?

'Why did you choose St Mark?'

'Will you do St Luke or St Matthew next?'

'Have you read *The Secret Gospel*?'

'Have you read *Counterfeit or Genuine*? It's about the authenticity of the last twelve verses.'

'Have you read *Jesus in the First Three Gospels*?

'Will you come out to supper?'

'Can I interview you in depth?'

'Will you talk to our club?' 'Our group?' 'Our society?'

'Are you religious?' 'Are you a believer?' 'Are you a Christian?'

'Isn't it tiring?'

– Yes, it is!

After the visitors, there was a celebratory end-of-season party.

I had a comforting talk with Emlyn Williams, who was to follow me into the Playhouse Theatre with his solo performance of the short stories of Saki. He has the greatest experience of any performer of one-man-show touring. He advised me to be firm, and turn down all requests from the local luminaries to 'meet a few people after the show'. 'Let us know if you'd like us to show you around.' 'Talk to the students.' 'Let us give you a party – nothing formal – just some wine and cheese . . .', etc., etc., etc.

I fear his advice arrived too late!

Mercifully, the next day – Monday – was a day off. In the morning I cancelled engagements, and awaited a highly recommended doctor.

He was a very very old man, and did not inspire confidence. We spent the first ten minutes searching in his bag for a thermometer – without success. He said calmly, 'I must have lost it.' Then he asked me my symptoms and I told him of my congested chest, and the fact that after my recitals I was often deaf.

The doctor was deaf himself, and shouted back at me, 'What?'

'Deaf!'

'You're what?'

'Deaf!!'

'DEAD?'

'NO! DEAF!!'

'Oh . . . Take your shirt off!'

He examined me, told me I should not be working, gave me a

massive penicillin injection, gave me prescriptions for cortisone and ampicillin, and started to leave without packing his bag. I recovered his syringe and some bottles. It was a bitter-cold day and I told him he should be wearing a coat. He shouted boastfully, 'Never wear one!' and walked into a cupboard. Finally I guided him to the elevator and he went on his indomitable way.

After the injection, and a lot of pills, I felt psychologically better and decided to join friends for a wonderfully sedated dinner.

I also decided to keep a record of the following three weeks.

*

November 14th

Keith Waggoner, my quiet Kansan stage-manager, collected me at the hotel, and we travelled to Princeton in a limousine. Great relief to be out of New York. To the Nassau Inn. My suite was not ready, so we went for a walk. It's very pretty – but the Alexander Hall where I play seems to have been designed by Charles Addams. Many of the seats are totally hidden.

I rested in the afternoon – feeling woozy with the large doses of cortisone and ampicillin.

In my warm-up speech before the recital, I told the people sitting behind huge pillars and in concealed alcoves to pretend they were listening to the radio. It was one of the liveliest audiences of the tour, and at the end there was an immediate standing ovation.

Afterwards we went for a drink at the Tap Room of the hotel, where some very overweight young men and women were singing 'Roll Out the Barrel' and 'It's a Long Way to Tipperary'.

November 15th

In the Princeton University Art Museum is a terrifying painting called 'Christ Before Pilate' by Hieronymus Bosch. One of the soldiers has a ring through his nose. And all of the deliverers of Christ look like pigs.

I had lunch with a nice girl called Louise Erlich who was working on props and armour with the Prospect Company during *Antony and Cleopatra* and who is now working here at the McCarter Theatre. She kindly brought me a present of a small cushion made, but never used, for *Antony and Cleopatra*. The colour and fabric were the same as one of Antony's costumes – and depressed me the moment I saw it. I tried thanking her sincerely – but was actually thinking how I could lose it.

After the performance a stocky young man rushed at me outside the dressing-room, and asked whether doing *St Mark* had changed my life. Then he asked me *how* it had changed my life. Then, startlingly, he asked me: 'What's your name?' I said: 'Haven't you got a programme?' He said: 'No.' He'd arrived forty minutes late. He said: 'My name's Robert.' I said: 'Well, my name's Alec.'

There were several people watching this encounter – and I felt very self-conscious. I told him to get further details from my stage-manager, and fled to the privacy of my dressing-room.

Then a reporter from the *Washington Post* interviewed me in the hotel Tap Room.

November 16th

Drove to a field just outside Princeton, climbed into a chartered six-seater Piper aircraft, took off immediately, and flew in an hour to Worcester, Massachusetts. So simple! Unfortunately, because the plane was unpressurized, and my congestion still bad, when we landed I was almost totally deaf.

We were met by a Father William Van Etten Casey ('Call me Bill!'), a Jesuit priest, who drove us to a Howard Johnson's Motor Lodge. He also took us to lunch, and was very beguiling. But I was desperately worried about my ears. It was two weeks since I had seen the ear specialist in New York and things seemed to be getting worse.

I went to the theatre at the College of the Holy Cross at 6.30 to check the lighting and furniture and try out the acoustics, and realized that I couldn't hear my own voice. A student tried to find medical help – but it was useless.

I shut the dressing-room door, got down on my knees and prayed.

Then I lay on my back.

I felt better.

In the wings, as I stood waiting to go on, my ears seemed to be back to normal. I got through the recital, went straight to my Howard Johnson's bed with a glass of milk, and slept for ten hours.

November 17th

Bill Casey, the sixty four-year-old Jesuit priest and professor, picked me up at Howard Johnson's and took me for a drive.

We had lunch at a beautiful Colonial Inn – The Publick House at Sturbridge – and I had a fish called broiled pollock. Every hour and a half an alarm would go off in Father Bill's pocket and he said, 'That's the end of another class!' He had evidently cancelled his classes for the day in order to be with me. On the way back to Howard Johnson's, he told me what he had once said to John Gielgud and Alec Guinness, and that he didn't think that Siobhan McKenna could play whores. I will never understand Catholic priests.

November 18th

After a dreadful breakfast, served by a girl with an enormous dirty bandage wrapped round her seemingly severed hand, Bill Casey drove us to the airport and we flew to New York.

There was a two-hour wait and I sat quietly and read John Fowles's *Daniel Martin* – which is lasting the whole trip.

Then we boarded a plane for Minneapolis, and my heart sank when the pilot said we were going to fly very high. Sure enough, when we landed I was deaf again.

We were met by Dennis Babcock, the 'Special Events Producer' of the Guthrie Theatre. There was snow on the ground. We booked into L'Hotel de France (which claims to be the only French hotel in the United States) and had a wonderful dinner. Then Dennis took us to the Guthrie to see a production of *Boy meets Girl*. The play was not very good – although I liked the acting of Cara Duff-McCormick and W. H. Macy – but the theatre is marvellous. I think it is the most exciting theatre in the world.

After a drink with some of the company, I went to bed with my cloth ears, and tried to prepare a special warm-up speech for Minneapolis.

November 19th

Before doing *St Mark* at the Guthrie Theatre, I told a story about my audition for Tyrone Guthrie in 1954, and added that I wished that Guthrie could once more 'come striding down the aisle, snapping his fingers, full of ideas, and shake us all up'.

After the performance there was a wine and cheese party and

everybody seemed to have a Tony Guthrie story. Keith and I finally escaped, and had a martini and some onion soup at L'Hotel de France, and marvelled at the clear-skinned, healthy, happy mid-westerners around us.

I was asked to sign the celebrity book by the young manager. He showed me the previous page with the signatures of the Rolling Stones. He said, 'We were quite surprised by Mick Jagger. He came in to eat all by himself, and looked quite old and tired.' – And, like me, he probably had trouble with his ears.

November 20th

An old friend, Charles Nolte, who is a professor at the University here, took me to lunch. Then, as he had a class, he drove me to his house, lit a fire, showed me how to work the record player, and left me to snooze on the sofa with a blanket. I played Elgar's First Symphony and snoozed. It was delicious.

My cold is still dreadful, but I managed not to cough and enjoyed the performance. Afterwards there was a dinner party with one of the directors of the Guthrie, enlivened by Alvin Epstein and Marthe Schlamme.

November 21st

Saw an appalling matinée performance of *A Christmas Carol*. This is evidently the sixth consecutive year they have done the play, and forty performances are completely sold out. Why?!

Non-sequitur.

There is something spooky about the happy healthy midwest . . .

In New York people just say: 'Have a good day!'

Here, they say, 'You have a good day now!' as if they might smack you if you don't!

And they are all so young.

Are the old people locked up?

There is a feeling of a secret society.

November 22nd

Woke up at 4 a.m. in a state of excitement. Put on the light and did some writing. Got up at 5.30, and Dennis drove us to the airport.

Flew to Washington and we were met by a White House car – with a silent driver wearing sinister tiny dark glasses.

Checked in at the Hay Adam Hotel and met Larry Bussard (my New York stage-manager) and friends Gil Parker and Jimmy McDonald in the lobby. After unpacking, Keith, Larry and I walked over to the White House, identified ourselves, and met Gretchen Poston, the Social Secretary. We inspected the East Room – where I was to perform – and it looked lovely. The only problem was that there was no lighting for the little stage. There were three huge chandeliers, but they would light the audience more than me. Since the television newsmen would be bringing special lighting equipment with them, we decided to see if we could improvise something later in the day. I left Keith and Larry, and went to find lunch at the Sheraton Carlton Hotel, where I met Ed Wilson who had interviewed me earlier in the year for the *Wall Street Journal*.

After lunch, for the first time in my sheltered life, I had my hair cut by a girl. She did a good job. With my constant bronchial cough and *Mark* fatigue, I looked very plain and drawn and pale.

Then I went to rest at the hotel.

It was impossible. I was very nervous.

I thought that the unusual circumstances and surroundings would make me lose concentration.

I thought that I would make a total fool of myself.

I thought the performance would be abandoned.

I imagined headlines: 'British Actor Collapses At White House'.

My dreams of failure became increasingly ambitious until I shouted, 'Why are ye so fearful? How is it that ye have no faith?' and I had a bath and dressed.

Keith and Larry called for me in their smart suits – bought especially for the occasion. We drove to the White House, which was now floodlit, and walked up the famous front steps.

They had fixed the lighting in the East Room with a couple of spotlights, and I had a little rehearsal.

Then Larry and Keith took me to the Housekeeper's Office, which was to be my dressing-room, and I had a cup of tea.

Soon after 6.30 Gretchen took me upstairs to meet the President and Mrs Carter. I had the usual reaction to seeing world famous people for the first time: 'Why, they're no bigger than me!' Indeed, President Carter seemed to be a very slight man.

They greeted me warmly and, perhaps to put me at my ease, the President said, 'I was talking to your Prime Minister on Sunday. I told him you were coming by to do the Gospel. And he said, "Oh! *we* must have him over sometime!"'

I said, 'Thank you for acting as my P.R. man, Mr President.'

I told him that I had first done *St Mark* at Newcastle, and he spoke enthusiastically of his visit there.

He asked me whether I had considered doing any of the other Gospels, and he told me that, in preparation for the occasion, he had read St Mark's Gospel the previous evening.

To Alec McCowen,

Jimmy Carter

Rosalynn Carter

The White House again – myself with the President, and Mrs Carter

Then Gretchen Postern said that it was time for us to go in.

Mrs Carter protested that their young daughter, Amy, was not ready.

But Gretchen insisted that we must begin, took me by the arm and led me away whispering, 'We can't wait for Amy!'

President Carter called out, 'Alec!' I turned round and he said, 'Is there anything special you'd like me to say?' I said, 'I leave it to you, sir.' I walked into the East Room and sat on a seat reserved for me in the front row. I found myself next to a writer who had interviewed me in New York and we chatted. Then a voice said: 'The President of the United States,' and everyone stood up. I noticed that Amy had in fact arrived and was sitting between Mrs Carter and Miss Lillian, the President's mother.

The President introduced the performance to the audience – which consisted of two hundred religious leaders and their wives.

He introduced me – and got my name right!

Then I shook his hand, and stepped on to the little stage.

I said: 'For the first time on this tour of America of my recital from memory of St Mark's Gospel, I feel safe. I have the President as my prompter,' and there was a good laugh.

I spoke of my two grandfathers, wishing that they were alive and could be present, saying that one was a politician and the other a preacher, and contrasting their reactions to my being an actor.

Then I did my set introduction of *St Mark*, and at a certain planned moment, the cameramen stopped their work and left the room, the television lights went out, the doors were closed, my lights came on and the recital began.

It was hard work at first.

The audience seemed very subdued – apart from Amy who was very restless. I could plainly see the President and Mrs Carter try to quieten her, but she was obviously very tired and found her seat uncomfortable.

She wriggled a great deal.

I hoped that she would not stay for the second half.

She didn't.

During the interval, as I went back to the Housekeeper's Office to have my usual cough and spit into the wash basin, the audience were given apple juice or coffee, and an orchestra played.

In the second half of the recital I felt relaxed and gave a good concentrated performance.

When it was over, the President stood up and led a standing ovation. Then he thanked me warmly from the stage. I was introduced to other members of the family and we walked out together.

Then, while the President and Mrs Carter greeted every single member of the audience, I went downstairs and changed my clothes, and had a massive gin.

Knowing the President's attitude to hard liquor, I then gargled with Listerine and went into the dining-room.

At dinner we had roast beef, pumpkin pie and iced water.

I sat between President Carter and some of his oldest friends and, with the relief of having the performance over, I had to restrain myself from being over-boisterous. The occasion suddenly seemed like a crazy dream, and I felt as if the people were cartoon characters. Greer Garson was also at the table – which added to the feeling of unreality. Six violinists came into the room and unexpectedly played a selection from *Fiddler on the Roof*.

A message was handed to the President and I shamelessly tried to read it. I think it said: 'Ring Cyrus Vance: Urgent!' He left the table, and Mrs Carter leant over and held my hand while she talked with me and her friends.

When the President returned he murmured to her, 'We must leave!' and she went to get her coat.

At the request of the lady next to me, the President called a photographer and several photographs were taken.

Then Mrs Carter returned, goodbyes were said, and they walked out of the room on to the lawn, got into a helicopter and flew away.

The leaders of the Church and other members of the audience began to descend on me. I was absolutely exhausted and murmured to Keith to get me out.

The Senator from Honolulu invited me to visit.

A lady journalist told me I said 'Peace, be still' too quickly, and then demonstrated how it should be done: 'Peeeeeace, be stiiiiill.'

A Baptist leader got me in a vice-like grip and told me: 'Jesus thanks you.'

Finally I managed to get away.

Back at the hotel I thought I would collapse, and Greer Garson told me to go straight to bed with a hot drink. But I had a ten-minute lie-down, and then slipped out with my friends Gil Parker and Jimmy McDonald and had a blessed quiet drink with them. Later we were joined by several of the others, and the evening ended happily.

November 23rd

Had breakfast with Gil and Jimmy. At ten o'clock Keith and I

were driven to Dulles Airport in a White House car to catch the
11.10 plane to Denver.

It was the wrong airport.

Keith had made a mistake.

It was 10.45 and a keen young cab driver said he could get us
to the other airport in time.

At 11 o'clock we were stopped by a cop for speeding.

At 11.10 the cop was still taking notes. When he finally let us
go, we decided to go back to Dulles.

The day lurched to a complete standstill.

It was Thanksgiving. The airport was practically deserted.

We discovered another flight to Denver – making three stops
en route – leaving at 1.45 by Ozard Airlines, but this would
mean that we would miss our connection to Aspen.

Our tickets for the entire tour had to be rewritten. This took
an hour and a half.

I started to drink Bloody Marys.

Keith made phone calls to Aspen and Denver.

I read the papers.

Richard Coe in the *Washington Post* wrote:

> The nation's most historic room had another 'first' last
> night. In the White House East Room, where Abigail Adams
> hung the second first family's laundry, where martyred
> Abraham Lincoln lay in state and where 15 years ago today
> John F. Kennedy was also lying in state, a rare, rich-voiced
> British actor, Alec McCowen, presented his celebrated
> readings of St Mark's Gospel.
>
> It was impossible to separate the performance – the actor's
> impeccably memorized, two-hour reading of the entire
> Gospel – from the great room itself.
>
> In the first row President Carter, who said that he had read
> the scripture straight through the night before, proved to be
> the actor's perfect audience. The President caught each shade
> of detail the actor's skill revealed. 'He anticipated the
> audience,' McCowen said later.
>
> It is a remarkable performance, not for its memory work
> but for its revelation that the shortest gospel is a miracle of
> narrative drive and for the clear beauty of the King James
> Version. Such language so eloquently used will be one more
> memory of the haunted salon.

In another paper the President's mother was reported as saying she thought the evening was 'two hours too long'.

Strangely, because of the strain of the past days, I felt very relaxed. It was just wonderful to have a day off.

Then the journey started and we flew slowly to Denver against strong head winds, stopping at Champaign Urbana, Peoria, and Sioux Falls.

Night fell.

At Denver, since there was no connecting flight to Aspen, we were met by a splendid no-nonsense lady called Ann B. Davis, who was a friend of someone, and who had offered to drive us into the mountains.

She said it would only take four and a half hours.

I took the back seat and had a gorgeous sleep.

We arrived at Aspen, Colorado, at 10.30 (having gained two hours) and were whisked off to have Thanksgiving Dinner.

I wasn't sure who anybody was, but I had a very good time, and they were very nice.

November 24th

Woke up in a Ski Lodge in a bedroom with a wall-to-wall ceiling mirror. Keith made coffee.

The height of the town combined with the Thanksgiving drinks had given me a headache, and I was coughing violently.

But the strangeness of the surroundings – luxurious log cabin, leather furniture, the mountains outside, and the quiet after the long journey – was delicious.

Keith made a fire and we watched a rota of local advertisements on TV.

'Gay Aspen Lives! Ring 7463.'

'*St Mark's Gospel*. Tonite at 8 p.m.'

'Fashion Fever Disco.'

And so on . . .

Then Bob Murray, our presenter in Aspen, arrived with a definitely English lady called Angela from Cheltenham, and they took me for a drive.

I discovered that Aspen is a cultural centre, and is inhabited by many people who have decided to leave the cities and lead the spacious unpolluted life. Old buildings are preserved; many artists, writers and composers live there; and the skiing tourists are tolerated for the money they bring into the little town.

The theatre was charming.

There was an oxygen machine in the wings in case I should need it.

The excitement over the performance was very flattering. Afterwards there was a champagne party and I flirted shamelessly with everybody.

November 25th

Aspen sparkled in the sun and snow. Bob Murray collected us, and we had Eggs Benedict in a crowded restaurant.

Why can't we make Eggs Benedict properly in England?

We visited an art gallery, and then drove to the little airport.

Then we had another hard day's flying.

We flew to Denver, and changed planes.

We flew to Atlanta, and changed planes.

We flew to Melbourne, Florida. It was 11.30 p.m. when we arrived.

We were met by our presenter Nancy McLarty and her friend Rosemary Smathers, and taken to Vero Beach.

Nancy McLarty is an old friend, and she has been inviting me to stay with her for many years. Now, by organizing two performances of *St Mark* at her local theatre, I finally saw her beautiful home.

November 26th

Woke up in the guest bungalow beside a swimming-pool and a golf course in Florida.

Sunshine.

Bougainvillaea, hibiscus, oleanders.

Nancy showed me the way through her lush forest of Pepper Trees, Coconut Palms, Christmas Palms, Banana Plants and Australian Pines to the ocean, and I walked straight into the sea.

She cried out, 'Watch the undertow!'

Later, Nancy introduced me to her mother, Dodo McLarty, a monumental eighty-two-year-old Southern matron. She was also concerned about the undertow and instructed me firmly never to swim without a lifeguard. As I left her presence, she barked out the wonderful Southern phrase: 'You heah me?!' and I said meekly, 'Yes, ma'am!'

I had a wonderful day in the sun and, for a time, I went into a coma of relaxation as if I was drugged.

The Vero Beach audience was very respectful.

Afterwards, Nancy introduced me to about fifty people who were congregated in the wings.

I met the Press.

Then we went off to a splendid restaurant called The Ocean Grill which had stayed open especially for the occasion. Bob Hosman and Mark Steinberg, my friends from Florida, joined us.

After only one day in the sun I felt better.

At two in the morning I walked alone through the forest garden to the beach. The trees and vegetation looked white in the moonlight. People seemed to be everywhere . . . but they were only shadows.

November 27th

Nancy has two black maids, called Willie Mae and Mamie, and when I met them yesterday they were very shy and did not speak. They came to *St Mark* last night, and today they are like old friends. Willie Mae greeted me: 'That was the most fantastic thing I ever saw!' and Mamie said, 'That was the best thing that I've ever seen!'

Right on!

I walked along the sand for a couple of miles.

This is one of the great pleasures of life.

Sea and sun, a breeze, and no destination.

November 28th

Day off.

In the evening Nancy and her friends Rosemary and Em took us to their club. Nancy said, 'The people at the next table could probably buy Florida.' After dessert we looked at a display of jewellery which made the Crown Jewels look like miniatures, and at the yachts moored outside.

It was a relief to get back to my bungalow and unexpectedly see The Two Ronnies on television. Good Old English lavatory jokes . . .

November 29th

I was very touched that Dodo McLarty had got up early to see me off. She presented me with some cough sweets.

We got into Nancy's Cadillac and drove away.

Then we flew to Atlanta, changed planes and flew to Norfolk, Virginia.

Here, we met Hatcher Story.

We had been looking forward to this meeting.

Hatcher Story is a peanut farmer from Franklyn, Virginia, who had read about my recital of St Mark's Gospel early in the summer, and contacted Arthur Cantor immediately. He had threatened Arthur that if I didn't come to Franklyn, Virginia, he would personally come to New York with a crate of chickens and let them loose in Arthur's office.

He had sent me photographs of his farmhouse.

He had offered to move out of his farmhouse during my visit and live with his sister, leaving me in possession.

He had sent me a large menu of local dishes to choose for our dinner.

He had sent me a giant tin of home-cooked salted peanuts, 'selected Jumbos', with a note saying: 'Everyone in this Peanut Country is looking forward to hearing you on 29 November.'

He had asked me to make out a list of a dozen friends in England, and offered to send them peanuts for Christmas.

Waiting for us at the barrier was a gentle giant of a man in a battered hat, grinning from ear to ear. He was sixty-two years old; gnarled faced, clear blue eyes.

He greeted us like long-lost relatives, and we drove to the little town of Franklyn; population, 10,000.

Outside the shopping centre was a sign saying, 'Welcome Alec McCowen'. On the other side of the sign it said, 'Turkey Shoot Tonite'.

We dropped Keith at Franklyn High School where I was to play, and Hatcher drove me to his little farmhouse.

There was a white peacock on the roof and enormous turkeys in the yard.

It was pouring with rain.

Hatcher made me tea, and I took a shower.

At Franklyn High School, I dressed in the music-room with three tubas.

The auditorium was packed. Hatcher is obviously popular in the town because they roared with laughter before the recital when I mentioned The White House and said that I had also played for 'the *other* peanut farmer'.

Afterwards, after meeting many townsfolk and a St Mark's Gospel group from Richmond, we went back to the farmhouse. Hatcher had read in an interview of my love of American Martinis, and he had been practising for weeks. We had a few.

I met Hatcher's cook, Ollie Mae – who had been to the recital and said she wanted 'to shout out several times'.

She had prepared a feast.

Southampton Virginia ham.

Chicken, with Ollie Mae's own celery sauce.

Corn pudding.

Turnip greens with smoked sausages.

Candied yams with marshmallows.

Alfalfa sprout salad with avocado . . .

. . . followed, at my request, with

Prune pudding.

I staggered to bed.

November 30th

Woke up in a timbered farmhouse bedroom, with chickens, turkeys and peacocks strutting around outside.

Hatcher arrived and made breakfast. Then he took us to a shop called The Peanut Patch where I met many local ladies, and was presented with a silver peanut paperweight.

Hatcher was pleased and proud that everything had gone well, and started to plan further visits.

He drove us to the James River Ferry, discovered we had an hour to wait, and we all went to sleep in the car.

Then we visited the wonderfully reconstructed Colonial town of Williamsburg, and had lunch in an English Inn.

It was a great twenty-four hours, and I left my heart in Franklyn, Virginia.

We flew to Philadelphia. Here, we were met by a handsome pink-eyed young professor. He greeted me, and I introduced Keith.

He said, 'Hello, Kath!'

I said, 'No! Keith!'

He said, 'Oh yes! Kath – I mean Keith – sorry, I've been drinking.'

He looked around vaguely and said, 'I've got a friend here who's waiting for another fly.'

I said, 'What?'

He said, 'I mean, he's waiting for another flight. We weren't sure which one you were on.'

We met his friend, another young professor, who had also been drinking.

We found our luggage and got into a large station wagon.

They didn't seem very sure of the way.

They asked if I would like to stop off for a drink at their favourite bar but, although they were very funny, I was exhausted and refused.

We arrived at St David's Inn. I took a Mogadon and slept for eleven hours.

December 1st

We are back in suburbia. In the morning Keith and I went for a walk round a supermarket and three car parks. I slept some more in the afternoon, and the handsome young professor drove me to Rosemont College for the performance. He was now completely sober and very considerate.

During the day, Michael Lindsay Hogg, the theatre and television director, had arrived from England to see the performance. He brought loving messages from Penelope Keith, Charles Kay and Nigel Hawthorne. He is to direct the television production of *St Mark*.

After the show – with a splendid audience – we looked in briefly at a college reception, and then went to eat and talk. Michael is stimulating, charming and very clever. We were both full of ideas, and I reinforced my determination not to do the television in front of an audience but to completely re-think the performance, telling the story to the camera.

December 2nd

We flew to Dallas on a plane that seemed to be full of giant men and women and on our arrival we were immediately told that Dallas Airport is larger than the island of Manhattan.

Then things started to go wrong.

Our presenter, an actor, Randy Moody, had arranged for us to see the current production at the theatre, but we had already accepted an invitation to dinner. He was hurt, and obviously slightly angry.

At the Hyatt Regency Hotel – where the lobby is eighteen

storeys high and the elevators go up and down like yo-yos – they lost my luggage.

When it was finally found, we tried to go to our dinner engagement but there was a disorganized crowd of noisy people outside the hotel waiting for taxis. There were very few taxis, and the trick seemed to be to tip the doorman an enormous sum.

I don't think he liked my accent.

We kept being pushed aside.

Keith, the quiet Kansan, suddenly got mad and seized a limousine, scattering a crowd of people in evening dress and shouting down the doorman. I was very proud of him. I would have given up.

Then the limousine driver couldn't find our address . . .

. . . Forget 2 December!

December 3rd

Woke up on the twentieth floor of the Hyatt Regency, with four motorways, a railway, and the flat Texan horizon outside the window.

It is Sunday, and at least two of the television channels seem to have continuous religious programmes. Among them I saw a 'miracle service' in which a man was curing a line of people with broken ear drums. After the miracle he would say, 'You can hear!' They would say, 'I can hear!' He would say, 'Who did it?' and they would say, 'The Lord did it!' and the audience applauded. While I was watching, he also cured a few people with cataracts and one alcoholic.

On another programme, attractive young singers – who reminded me of Dickie Valentine and Lita Rosa in the Fifties – sang lyrics like:

> There's a joy in giving,
> And I've found it to be true,
> The more you give to Jesus,
> The more he gives to you.

Everyone was fantastically laundered and shampooed, and very very happy.

In the gift shop of the hotel they sell postcards of the place where John Kennedy was shot, with arrows indicating where the shots were fired.

On the way to the theatre we passed this place. And before

and during the recital of *St Mark* the assassination was in my mind.

In a sense Dallas is like Golgotha: 'the place of a skull'. And the tragedy of Kennedy has the proportions of a modern-day crucifixion.

Perhaps this awareness made the recital the most positive that I have given.

December 4th

A day off in Dallas.

Keith and I went out and had a 'Country Boy Breakfast' in a little restaurant where the menu said: 'Tell us how you like yore aigs 'n' loosen yore belt.'

Then we went to the famous store Neiman-Marcus and tried on cowboy hats.

We saw the newly placed Henry Moore sculpture outside the City Hall, sat in the sun and looked at people looking at it.

We went up Reunion Tower – an absurd Christmas-tree ball revolving in the sky – and drank Harvey Wallbangers.

And in the evening we had dinner with Greer Garson and her husband, Buddy Fogelson.

December 5th

Randy Moody drove us to the airport, and we flew to St Louis.

My name was up in lights outside the American Theatre. This is a proper 'touring date', and we are here for the whole week.

My deafness has cleared up, but the congestion in the chest lingers; and at every performance I worry that I shall start coughing and not be able to stop.

While in St Louis I saw another specialist, but he said that there was nothing he could do for me.

I think I need a bit of a rest.

I need my own bed.

I need to belt up.

*

This diagnosis was confirmed in December when I got back to England. I was told that there was nothing wrong with me, except that I was in a state of exhaustion. They said the symptoms were warning signs, and that I should take a good rest.

Just before Christmas, on the invitation of the Dean of Westminister, I did *St Mark's Gospel* in Westminster Abbey for a charity performance. The acoustics in the Abbey are dreadful, but Geoffrey Yates, of Christian Audio, once again managed to make me audible. I dressed in the Jerusalem Chamber, where the King James Version was translated. My waiting-room was Edward the Confessor's Chapel in the very heart of the Abbey. They gave me a little chair by Richard II's tomb, and they asked me not to sit on the Stone of Scone on the Coronation Chair, or a loud alarm would go off all over the Abbey. Strangely, it was not an over-awing experience, but reminded me of being in my old village church in Langton Green, Kent.

In January, as a final coincidence, I performed both *Hadrian VII* and *St Mark's Gospel*. I did a radio version of *Hadrian* at Broadcasting House, directed by Martin Jenkins. Then I did the television version of *St Mark*, directed by Michael Lindsay Hogg.

Once again, Hadrian seemed to be the most gorgeous and rewarding role. Once again, I took delight in the dazzling invective. Once again, I enjoyed the scones and the raspberry jam and the yogurt in the canteen of Broadcasting House.

Then it was back to another bleak rehearsal room in Chiswick. At first, I was jealous of relegating my authority of *St Mark* to the director, the designer, the lighting man, and the camera and sound men. But Michael Lindsay Hogg, Anthony Cartledge, Andy Andrews, John Darnell, Peter Stoddart and Bob Davis soon became deeply involved in the project. The final four days in the studio at Thames Television were a remarkably dedicated time, and I thought that everybody did the best possible job. .

After the television production of *St Mark* was finished, I felt empty and exhausted. The thought of continuing with the recital seemed unattractive. The thought of doing *any* work seemed unattractive. Retirement was the only answer. I was played out . . .

. . . But then, as we used to say at the movies in the great days of continuous double-features: 'This is where we came in.'

And, as it happened, in February I rested.

In March I did a television version of *The Family Dance*.

And in April I crossed the Atlantic again and did *St Mark* at the University of Toronto; and also at the Eisenhower Theatre in the

Kennedy Center, Washington, where four years previously I had developed the psychosomatic throat and sat in my hotel room wrapped in a blanket.

*

There are a number of common elements to these theatrical stories of *Hadrian VII* and *St Mark's Gospel*. Of course, the most striking of these is the religious element. The fact that my work has led me into this area is a surprise to me.

I do not regard myself as a religious man.

It makes me very uneasy to be asked, 'Are you a Christian?'

It seems to me very unlikely that anyone – least of all oneself – can be a judge of this.

If there is any judging to be done, if there is any seal of approval, if there are any awards to be given, these must surely be based on behaviour as well as belief.

The joy of *Hadrian VII* is that it tells the story of a man who actually puts Christianity into practice – and thoroughly disconcerts the Christians.

The joy of *St Mark* is that it goes beyond the Crucifixion, and, in those last disputed verses, tells the story of the risen man rolling up his sleeves and instructing us: 'Go ye into all the world, and preach the gospel to every creature.'

I read somewhere – or heard somewhere: 'There cannot be any goodness unless it is practised goodness.'

But, personally, I do not think that I qualify either in the realms of belief or behaviour to be called a Christian.

In the last verse of St Mark we learn that the disciples 'went forth, and preached every where, the Lord working with them, and confirming the word with *signs following*'.

Certainly, when I was working on *St Mark* and performing *St Mark*, there were signs. On several occasions, when I least expected it and when I most needed it, there would be a sign.

I became aware that the sun, the moon, or even the glow from a burning candle, assumed a new significance.

Whenever I needed it, I was blessed; and blessed specifically with light and warmth.